CW01390109

International Baccalaureate
Physics
Astrophysics Option E

For examination in 2009

Introduction

Welcome to the International Baccalaureate Physics Guide to the Astrophysics Option. The author has 27yrs teaching experience, 17yrs of which have been teaching IB physics in international schools. The author studied astronomy at University College London, this being a good grounding for astrophysics.

This guide is not a textbook, as it does not cover every syllabus statement in detail. Its aim is to support your textbook and the notes made in class. This is achieved by summarising the key points, some two dozen worked examples each followed by similar problems. Also, there are several hands on tasks allowing students to improve their graphing skills, a list of the commonest mistakes in the exam and finally over fifty questions-split into core and higher level extension, all with answers. Have a calculator at hand, plus pencil and eraser to fill in the spaces, rub out and try again at a later date.

I would like to thank Jacek Latkowski for kindly proof-reading the manuscript and many students for letting me use them as guinea pigs for the booklet.

I would greatly value any feedback on this revision guide so that later editions can continue to help students round the world. Please feel free to email me at Oxford Study Courses-(osc@osc-ib.com).

Hugh Duncan

Contents

Common Core Topics

Introduction to the universe

<u>The structure of the solar system</u>

-the **solar system** is the collection of bodies that is gravitationally bound to the sun (planets, moons, asteroids and comets).
-the nine **planets** constitute the major bodies in the solar system. They go round the sun in elliptical orbits (most are almost circular).
-in order of increasing distance from the sun, they are Mercury, Venus, Earth, Mars, Jupiter, Saturn, Uranus, Neptune and Pluto.
-make up a mnemonic to remember the order eg:
Most Very Eminent Men Just Sleep Under New Planets (MVEMJSUNP)
-in order of increasing size, they are Pluto, Mercury, Mars, Venus, Earth, Uranus, Neptune, Saturn and Jupiter.
-the **moons** or natural satellites orbit the planets.
-between Mars and Jupiter there is a gap that is filled with many smaller bodies called **asteroids** or minor planets.
-**Comets** are of a mixture of ice, dust and gas, just a few km across. Most comets orbit the sun in parabolic orbits.

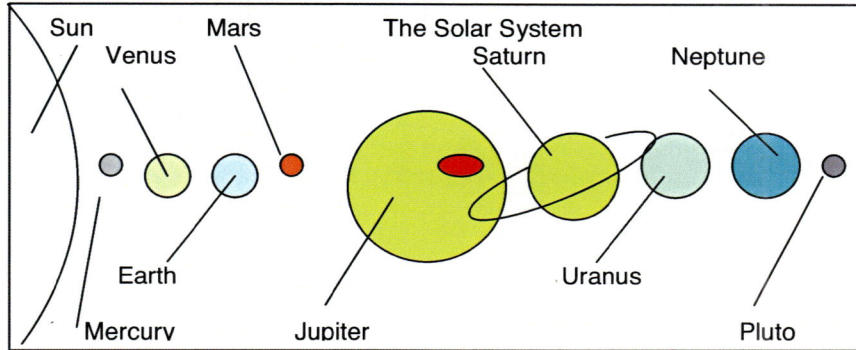

The Solar System
Sun, Venus, Mars, Saturn, Neptune, Earth, Uranus, Mercury, Jupiter, Pluto

Name	Diameter/km	Orbit radius/AU	Period
Mercury	4800	0.4	88d
Venus	12000	0.7	224d
Earth	13000	1.0	1y
Mars	6700	1.5	1.9y
Jupiter	142000	5.0	12y
Saturn	120000	9.5	29y
Uranus	49000	19	84y
Neptune	50000	30	164y
Pluto	1200	39	248y

<u>Star groups</u>

-a **galaxy** is a collection of 100 billion stars, dust and gas held together by gravity. They can be **spiral** shaped, or **elliptical** though some are **irregular**. Our galaxy, the Milky Way is spiral.
-within a galaxy a close group of bound stars is called a **cluster**. A **globular** cluster has about 10^5 stars symmetrically arranged and more densely packed in the centre. An **open** or moving cluster is irregular in shape with hundreds of stars.
-stars in the same part of the sky (but may be at different distances), are grouped together into shapes called **constellations**.
-consider distant street lights that make a pattern.
-they may be at different distances, but are in the same direction.

-the pair of diagrams below might help to show this.
-they each show the same constellation pattern of stars.
-however, if you cross your eyes and allow one image to merge with the other (this is a stereogram a bit like Magic Eye), it can be seen that one of the stars is further away than the others. Have a go!

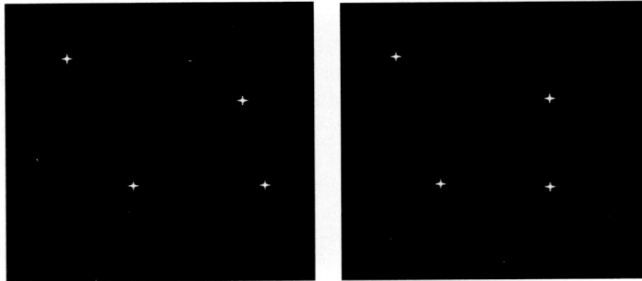

NB it's the top left one. Bottom right is nearest. If the stars weren't so far away or if our eyes were very far apart, we'd be able to see them at different distances!

The light year

A **light year** is the distance light travels in one year. Taking the speed of light as 3.0×10^8 ms^{-1}, 365 days in a year, 24 hrs in a day, 60 mins to an hour and 60 sec to a minute, a light year is equal to

$$1 \text{ ly} = 3 \times 10^8 \times 365 \times 24 \times 60 \times 60 = 9.46 \times 10^{15} \text{ m}$$

> 1. The moon is 370 000 km away. How long does it take light to travel form the earth to the moon? Note c is also 300 000kms^{-1}
> 2. How far away is the sun in light minutes if the distance is 150 000 000km? .
> 3. The closest star after the sun is Proxima Centauri, 4.3ly away. How far is this in metres? The fastest man made object reached 150 000 ms^{-1}. How long would it take it to travel to Proxima Centauri?
> 4. The most distant star visible to the naked eye is epsilon Aurigi at 5000ly. How far is this in m?
> 5. The most distant galaxy visible to the naked eye is the Andromeda Galaxy M31 at 2.2×10^6 ly. How far is this I metres?
> Answers, 1. 1.2s 2. 8.3min 3. 4.1×10^{16} m, 8600yrs! 4. 4.73×10^{18} m 5. 2.1×10^{22} m.

Comparing distances between stars and galaxies

-our galaxy the Milky Way contains about 10^{11} stars and is disk shaped about 100 000 ly across and 10 000 ly thick. The average distance between the stars is about 10 ly.

-assume a galaxy has a cuboid volume, 100 000 x 100 000 x 10 000ly giving a total volume of 10^{14} ly^3.
-as there are about 10^{11} stars that means each star has a volume to itself of $10^{14} / 10^{11} = 1000$ ly^3.
-assuming that volume is a cube then the side length of the cube will be cube root 1000, = 10 ly, so the mean spacing of stars in a galaxy is 10ly; this is many orders of magnitude greater than the actual size of the stars (a few light second across).

-Our galaxy is one of 20 galaxies in a cluster called the Local Group. The Local group's radius is about 2 million ly, the average distance between the galaxies is about a million ly.

Show that the mean distance between galaxies in a cluster is about 10^6 ly
Assume a cube of side length 4 million ly, giving a volume of 64 million ly^3 giving about 3.2 million ly^3 space for each galaxy so the cube root of this would give the size of the cube for a galaxy, which is about 1.4 million ly. As the diameter of a galaxy is of the order of 100 000 ly then the distance between them is only of the order of a magnitude greater.

-In comparison, the distance between clusters of galaxies is tens to hundreds of millions of light years. Our Local Group is in fact a 'satellite' cluster to the much larger Virgo super cluster, which contains many more galaxies.

Apparent motion of the stars

-the stars appear to take almost 24hours to go round the earth.
-the point they turn about is called the North celestial Pole
-The Pole Star Polaris is so close to the celestial pole, it doesn't appear to move.
-in reality it is the earth that is spinning on its own axis every 24h.
-the sun appears to move round the sky in 24h.
-the sun lags behind the stars, as the earth is orbiting the sun.
-it takes the sun a year to move against the stars.

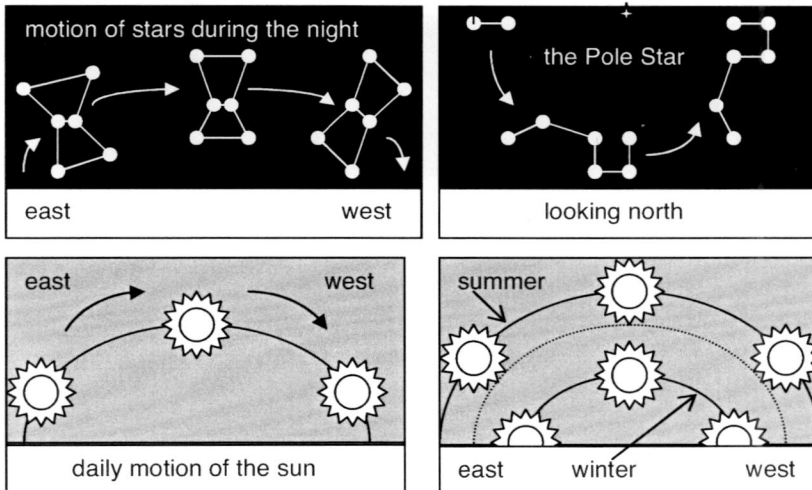

| motion of stars during the night | | the Pole Star |
| east | west | looking north |

| east | west | summer |
| daily motion of the sun | | east   winter   west |

Task box one: fill in the missing words numbered below into the spaces on the right, then check the answers on the next page.

(1).... the collection of bodies bound by gravity to the sun. (2) .... the smallest planet. (3) ... the furthest planet from the sun. (4)... bodies that orbit the planets. (5)... bodies found orbiting between Mars and Jupiter. (6)... small bodies made of dust gas and ice. (7) ... a large collection of stars bound by gravity, which can be either (8), (9), or (10). (11)... a large symmetrical collection of stars in a galaxy. (12).. a small irregular collection of stars in a galaxy. (13)... a set of stars making a pattern, seemingly close in the sky. (14).. the distance light travels in a year. The distance between stars in a galaxy is (15) compared to the stars. The distance between galaxies is (16) compared to the galaxies.

Task box 1

1. _____
_____
2. _____
3. _____
4. _____
5. _____
6. _____
7. _____
8. _____
9. _____
10. _____
11. _____
12. _____
13. _____
14. _____
15. _____
16. _____

Stellar radiation and stellar types

Stellar radiation, luminosity and apparent brightness

-the source of energy for the stars comes from **nuclear fusion**.
-four hydrogen atoms collide at speed to form helium
-energy is released in the form of radiation.
-the force of gravity is trying to collapse a star.
-the radiation created in nuclear fusion exerts an outward pressure on a star.
-the two forces, gravity and radiation pressure are in equilibrium, making a star stable.
-**luminosity** is the total power output of a star in watts
-the luminosity of a 100W light bulb is 100W!
-the luminosity of the sun is 3.9×10^{26} W.
-the **apparent brightness** of a star is the power output per unit area at a given distance and is measured in Wm^{-2}

If a star of luminosity L is observed from a distance d, then the apparent brightness b is given by

$$b = \frac{L}{4\pi d^2}$$

As an example, suppose you are standing 3m away from a 100W light bulb. Its apparent brightness given by the equation will be

$b = 100/4 \times 3.14 \times 3^2 = 0.9 \ Wm^{-2}$

> Worked example:
> Using the luminosity figure for the sun as 3.9×10^{26} W, its brightness as seen from the earth, at a distance of 1.5×10^{11}m can be found:
> $L = 3.9 \times 10^{26}$ W
> $d = 1.5 \times 10^{11}$m
> $b = 3.9 \times 10^{26}/(4 \times 3.142 \times (1.5 \times 10^{11})^2$
> $b = 1379 W/m^2 = 1400 Wm^{-2}$ (2 sig fig)
> Note this figure is known as the solar constant.
> What would the apparent brightness of the sun be at a distance of one light year?
> (Ans: $3.5 \times 10^{-7} \ Wm^{-2}$)

Black body radiation

Task box 1
ANSWERS

1. solar system.
2. pluto
3. pluto.
4. moons/ satellites
5. minor planets/ asteroids.
6. comets
7. galaxy
8.9.10. spiral, elliptical, irregular.
11.globular cluster
12. open/ moving cluster
13. constellation.
14. light year
15. large.
16. similar

-a **black body** is a body that is a perfect absorber and a perfect emitter of radiation.
-a star is an example of a black body.
-the relative amounts of each type radiation from a black body depends only on the surface temperature of the black body.
Below is a graph showing the intensity of radiation for three black bodies at different temperatures. The vertical axis is an arbitrary intensity unit, the horizontal axis is wavelength in nm.
As the surface temperature increases,
- there is an increase in all types of radiation
- there is a greater increase for shorter wavelength radiation.
- the peak of intensity shifts to shorter wavelengths

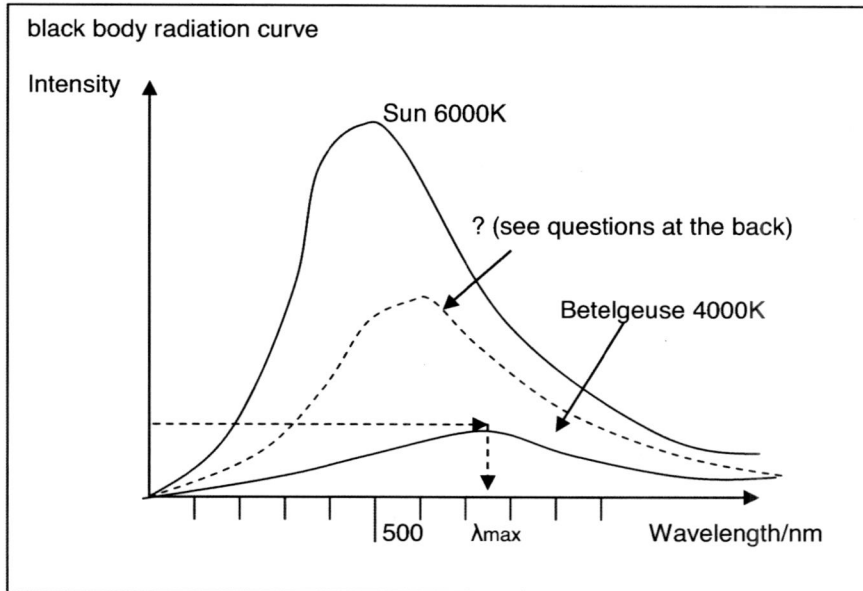

black body radiation curve

Intensity

Sun 6000K

? (see questions at the back)

Betelgeuse 4000K

500   λmax   Wavelength/nm

Worked example:
Betelgeuse has a surface temperature of about 4000K. Note from the graph that the radiation peaks at about 750nm. This is in the red part of the spectrum, so Betelgeuse looks red.
The sun has a surface temperature of about 6000K. Where does the radiation peak?
(Ans: 500nm, which is green, but the mixture of colours makes it look yellow)

Wien's and Stefan's Laws

-**Wien's displacement law** states that the wavelength at peak intensity for a black body is inversely proportional to the surface temperature.
-wavelength at max intensity = constant / temperature

$$\lambda\text{max} = \frac{0.00290}{T}$$

where λ is in m and T is the temperature in Kelvin.

-the colour of a black body indicates its temperature.
-this property is used to classify stars into groups or **spectral types.**

Worked example
The constant in Wien's law is 0.00290 Kelvin-metres (Km). If the spectrum of Betelgeuse peaks at 700nm, the quoted surface temperature can be found:
Constant = 0.00290 Km
Wavelength at max intensity = 700nm (change to metres!) = 7×10^{-7}m
Rearrange formula temp = constant / peak wavelength
Temp = $0.00290/7 \times 10^{-7}$m = 4142 = 4100K (2sf)
Using the wavelength at max intensity found earlier for the sun (500nm), calculate the surface temperature;
(Ans 5800K 2sf)

-the luminosity of a star is proportional to its surface area.
-the luminosity of a star is proportional to the fourth power of the surface temperature.
-this is called **Stefan-Boltzmann's law**
-for two different sized stars of the same temperature, the power output per unit area is the same.

The radiation rate is L (known as the power or luminosity) in watts
The surface temperature is T in Kelvin
The surface area is A in m²
The Stefan-Boltzmann formula is

$L = \sigma A T^4$

σ is Stefan's constant 5.7×10^{-8} $Wm^{-2}K^{-1}$.

Worked example:
Take the sun, where T = 6000K and its radius is 6.7×10^8 m. Find the power output.
T = 6000K $A = 4 \times \pi \times (6.7 \times 10^8)^2 = 5.64 \times 10^{18}$ m²
$\sigma = 5.7 \times 10^{-8}$ W/m²/K
$L = 5.7 \times 10^{-8} \times 5.64 \times 10^{18} \times 6000^4 = 4.16 \times 10^{26}$ W $= 4.2 \times 10^{26}$ W (2sf)
(Note this is approximately the number given earlier).
Sirius has a surface temperature of 13000K and a radius of 1.3×10^9 m. Find the power output.
(Ans: 3.5×10^{28} W)

Stellar spectra

-a pure gaseous element when heated or excited by a voltage gives out very specific wavelengths. If split up using a prism and emission line spectrum is seen
-a black body gives out radiation of all wavelengths. If split up with a prism a continuous spectrum is seen.
-if a continuous spectrum is shone through a gaseous element, the colours it would normally give out are absorbed and dark lines appear
-stars are not perfect black bodies as their thin atmospheres absorb certain colours and leave dark lines in the spectrum
-each element absorbs its own colours, so the dark lines in a star's spectrum allow the chemical composition of a star to be found.
-some physical properties of a star can be found with the spectrum.
-if the lines are blue shifted or red shifted (see below) then the stars motion towards us or away can be determined

Stellar groups

-the grouping of stars into spectral types is called **spectral classification**
-there are seven spectral types O B A F G K and M.
-they are remembered using Oh B A Fine Girl Kiss Me!
-the temperature decreases from O (40 000K) to M (4 000K).
-the colour changes from blue (O and B), white (A), yellow (F and G), orange (K) to red (M).
-each type is subdivided into ten subgroups numbered 0 to 9. The sun for example is a type G2 star.

Types of stars

Single-a star that is not bound by gravity to another, such as the sun.
Binary-two stars that appear close together in the sky and may be physically related.
Cepheid-a star that varies in brightness over a period of days, due to changes in size.
Red Giant-a star that had finished hydrogen burning and is using helium in the core. Very large with a low surface temperature.
Supergiant-a star heavy enough to fusion burn elements beyond carbon.
White Dwarf-a star of solar mass but planetary size with no more fusion energy, only gravitational.

Binary stars

-two stars close together in the sky, but not actually close together in space are called an **optical binary**.
-two stars that orbit one another, is called a **visual binary**.
-two stars orbiting each other where one passes in front of the other is called an **eclipsing binary**.
-a graph of the brightness of a star as it changes with time is called a **light curve**.

Below is a graph that shows how the brightness (in arbitrary units) of such a system will appear to change with time (days).

eclipsing binary system

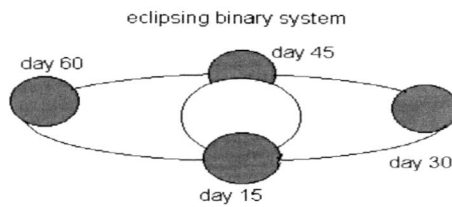

eclipsing binary light curve

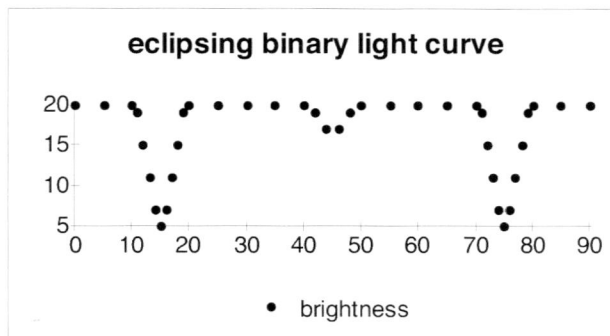

Task 2: time for another test. Below is a series of definitions with the key words removed. Fill in the blanks onto the answer grid on the right then check them against the mark scheme on the next page.

Task box 2

(1): the distance light travels in one year. (2); the source of energy for stars. (3); the power output in watts. (4); the power output per unit area at a given distance. (5); a perfect absorber and emitter of radiation. (6) law; the wavelength at peak intensity of the black body source is inversely related to surface temperature. (7) type or classification; the grouping of stars due to their surface temperature and colour. (8) law; the luminosity of a star depends on the fourth power of the surface temperature. (9) star; a star not bound by gravity to another. (10) star; two stars bound by gravity. (11); an unstable star that goes through periodic changes in brightness. (12); a star burning helium, the outer layers have expanded and cooled. (13); a star the size of the earth that has no fusion energy left, only gravitational. (14) binary; two stars close together in the sky. (15) binary; two stars bound by gravity and seen as two objects.(16) binary; a binary system where one star periodically passes in front of the other, cutting out some of the light. (17): the graph of a variable star's magnitude as it changes with time.

Task box 2
1. _____
2._____
3. _____
4.
_____
5. _____
_____
6. _____
7. _____
8. _____
9. _____
10. _____
11. _____
12. _____
_____
13. _____
_____
14. _____
15. _____
16. _____
17. _____
_____

Spectroscopic Binary

-some close binary stars show no eclipses.
-a spectrum of such a system will reveal two sets of lines, one from each star.
-such a system is called a **spectroscopic binary**.

Consider two stars A and B in a binary system (see diagram). At moment, one is moving towards us (position A1) and the other is moving away (B1). Due to the Doppler Effect, A will have the waves 'bunched up' and its lines shifted to the blue end of the spectrum. B's waves will be 'stretched out' and its lines shifted to the red end.

A quarter of a period later the stars move perpendicular to the line of sight (A2 and B2), so show no shift, creating only one set of lines.

A quarter of an orbit later the stars swap positions and two sets of lines appear again. The lines double then become single twice in each period. It is called a **spectroscopic binary** because the identity of the system can only be found using the spectra.

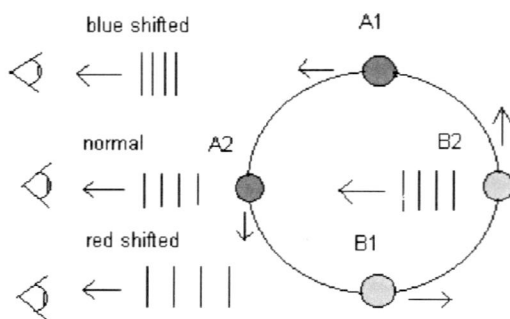

The Hertzsprung-Russell Diagram

-stars that have the same colour (same surface temperature) are in the same spectral class.

-stars of the same colour have the same power output per unit area.

-stars of the same spectral class can be very different in size (a red supergiant and red dwarf for example).

-a graph of a star's luminosity against its surface temperature is called a **Hertzsprung-Russell diagram** (HR diagram), see below.

-a more negative absolute magnitude means a more luminous star, so the y-axis is numbered in the reverse order to normal graphs.

-the x-axis, representing spectral type is numbered in order of decreasing temperature.

-NB, the scales on an HR diagram are not linear. Magnitude/luminosity is logarithmic,

> Task: from the table, plot each star onto the blank HR diagram, recalling that spectral types are split into sub groups 0 to 9 from left to right and absolute magnitude which represents luminosity is plotted 'upside down' with the more negative values at the top.

star	Sp	Mv	star	Sp	Mv
61 Cyg	K7	+8.4	Mintaka	O9	-6.1
Aldebaren	K5	-0.7	Mira	M6	-1.0
α Centauri A	G2	+4.4	Mirach	M0	+0.1
α Centauri B	K5	+5.7	Naos	05	-7.2
Altair	A7	+2.3	Polaris*	F8	-4.6
Ankaa	K0	+0.2	ProcyonB	F4	+13.0
Archenar	B5	-2.2	Procyon A	F5	+2.6
Barnards Star	M5	+13.2	Proxima	M5	+15.5
Betelgeuse	M2	-6.1	Sirius A	A1	+1.4
Delta Cephi*	F6	-3.6	Sirius B	A5	+11.8
Enif	K2	-4.6	Spica	B1	-3.4
Eta Cas b	M0	+8.7	Suhail	K5	-4.5
Kruger 60	M3	+11.9	Tau ceti	G8	+5.8
LP656-2	K5	+15.6	Wolf 28	G2	+14.3
Menkar	M2	-0.7	Wolf 359	M8	+16.7
Eta Oph	O9	-3.8	Gamma Vel	O5	-4.0
Alnitak	O9	-6.1	Alpheratz	B9	-0.9
Rigel	B8	-7.0	Alnilam	B0	-6.7
Beta Aur	A2	-0.2	Deneb	A2	-7.3
O Eri b	A5	+11.1	L145-141	A8	+13.0
Caph	F2	+1.5	Wezen	F8	-7.3
Scutulum	F0	-4.5	σ Pavo	G6	+4.8
Eta Psc	G8	+0.3	36 Oph	K1	+6.4
115636	K5	-4.4	Antares	M1	-4.4
Scheat	M2	-1.4	1326	M1	+10.3

Task 2
answers
1. light year
2. fusion
3. luminosity
4. brightness
5. black body
6. Wein's
7.spectral
8. stefan's
9. single
10. binary
11. Cepheid
12. red giant
13. white dwarf
14. optical
15. visual
16. eclipsing
17. light curve

Mv

-5

0

+5

10

15

| O | B | A | F | G | K | M |

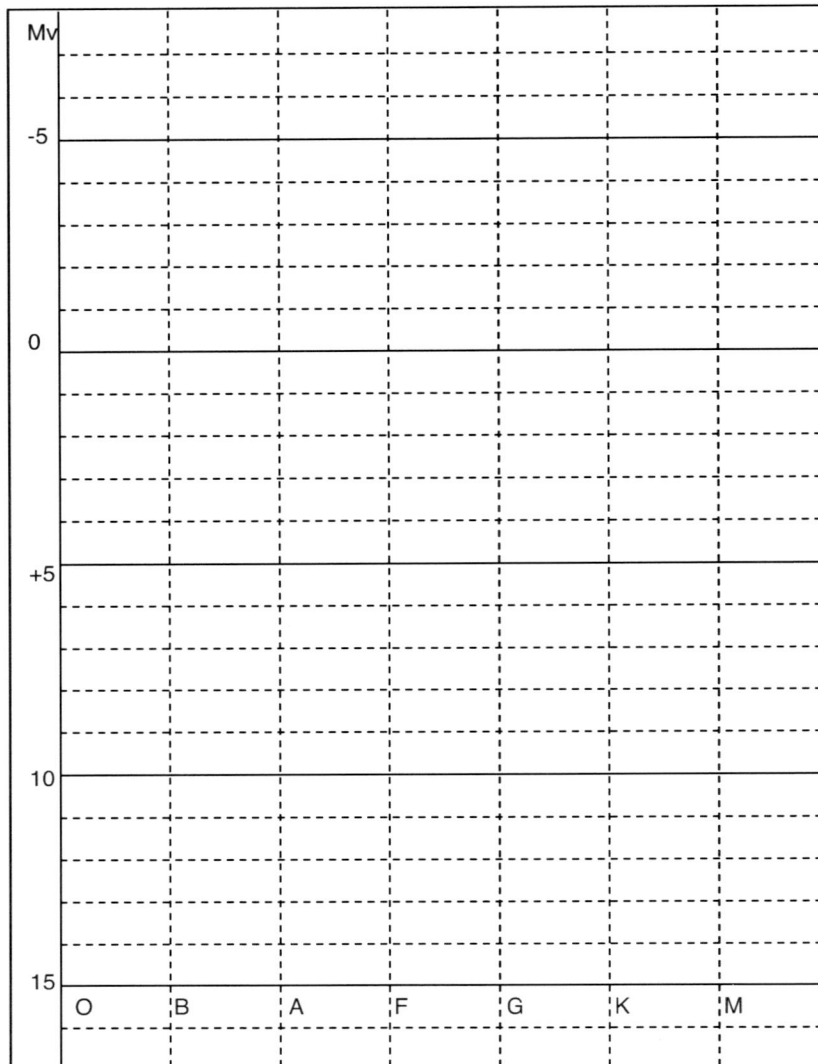

The main features of the diagram are:

-the **Main Sequence** (MS) runs from top left to bottom right.
-MS stars show a direct relationship between absolute magnitude (luminosity) and surface temperature.

-the sun is near the centre of the main sequence.
-MS stars are burning hydrogen by nuclear fusion to helium.
-heavier MS stars burn faster, look brighter, are hotter and bluer.
-lighter MS stars burn slower, are fainter, cooler, and look red.

-**Red Giants** stars have used up their hydrogen.
-their cores contract and heat up until helium burning starts, creating carbon.
-the outer layers expand and cool. The sun's evolution is shown.
-they are larger, more luminous and higher up on the HR diagram.

-**Supergiant** stars have used up the helium in their cores.
-their cores contract, heat up and carbon burning starts.
-the outer layers expand, helium burning continues in a shell.

12

-they are larger than the giants, luminous and higher on the diagram.

-Cepheids stars are giants that go through a period of instability.
-they oscillate in size, change temperature and luminosity.
-they are found between the main sequence and the giants.

-White dwarfs have no more nuclear fuel.
-gravity has overcome the radiation pressure contracting that star, heating up by converting gravitational energy to radiation. The sun's move is shown.
-they are earth-sized, faint and found below the main sequence.

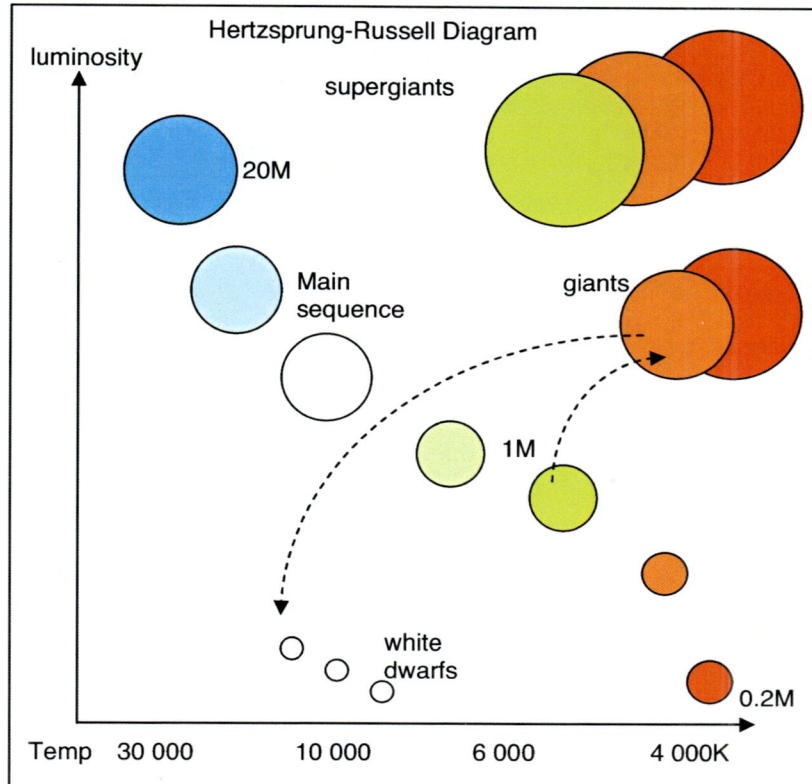

Note, a star's position on the main sequence depends on its mass, from 0.2 solar masses for the red end to 20 solar masses or more for the blue end.

Stellar Distances

Parallax method

-hold your finger up at arms length in front of you face.
-close one eye at look at the finger, then do the same with the other eye.
-your finger appears to move against the background.
-this is known as parallax.
-take the earth in two positions on its orbit six-months apart
-a nearby star is observed on those two dates (see diagram)
-its position relative to the distant stars will change.
-the angle of parallax, p is the difference in angular positions as seen from the earth and sun, measured in seconds of arc.
-the closer the star, the larger the parallax.

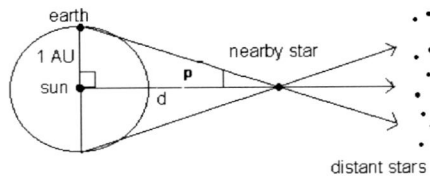

earth
1 AU
sun
p
d
nearby star
distant stars

Worked example:
α Centauri, the closest star has a parallax of 0.760 arcseconds. Using the triangle in the diagram, with the earth-sun distance as 1 astronomical unit 1 AU, this makes the distance to the nearest star (one degree is 60 minutes and one minute is 60 seconds, so one arc second is therefore 1/3600 of a degree) as:

Opposite/adjacent = tangent, so adjacent = opposite/tangent
d=1 AU/tan0.76 arc sec
which is about 271 000 AU. What is this in metres? In light years?
(Ans: 4.1 x 10^{16}m, or 4.3 ly)

-a **parsec** is the distance at which a star will have a parallax of 1 second of arc.

-the distance d in parsecs pc is $d = \dfrac{1}{p}$, where the parallax angle is given in arc seconds.

Worked example:
The nearest star has a parallax of 0.760 arc sec. What is this in parsecs?
Use d = 1/p, so d = 1/0.76, d = 1.3pc.
What is the distance when the parallax is 0.010 arc sec? 0.002 arc sec?
If the error in parallax is +/-0.001 arc sec, what error does this give for these distances?
(Ans: 100+/-10pc, 500+500/-200pc. NB error grows rapidly with distance)

-this method can only be used for stars within 100pc.
-beyond this, parallax is so small that the error is too large.

Apparent and absolute magnitudes

-stars appear not to have the same brightness, due to being at different distances and having different luminosities.
-the apparent magnitude of a star indicates the brightness as seen from earth.
-the lower (more negative) the magnitude, the brighter the star.

Worked example,
Aldeberan has a magnitude of 0.80 while Procyon is 0.36. Procyon is the brighter of the two as its magnitude is less positive (more negative).
Which is brighter, Sirius, magnitude −1.48 or Shaula +1.62?
(Ans: Sirius).

-the scale of magnitude is not linear. A change in brightness of a factor of one hundred is exactly fives magnitudes.

-a change of one magnitude represents a change in brightness of the fifth root of 100 or approximately 2.511.

> Worked example
> A two magnitude difference is a brightness difference of 2.511x2.511, or 2.511^2 which is about 6.25.
> What difference in brightness is three magnitudes? Four magnitudes?
> (Ans: 16, 40 approx)

-If two stars have apparent magnitudes of m_1 and m_2, and each brightness b_1 and b_2, then the brightness ratio b_2/b_1 is given by:

$$\frac{b_1}{b_2} = 2.511^{m_1-m_2}$$

> Worked example
> The Pole star has a magnitude 1.98, while Aldeberan is 0.80. How many times brighter does Aldebaren appear than the Pole Star?
> $m_1 = 1.98$
> $m_2 = 0.80$
> Use $b_2/b_1 = 2.511^{m_1-m_2}$
> $m_1 - m_2 = 1.98 - 0.80 = 1.18$
> So $b_2/b_1 = 2.511 \ 10^{1.18} = 2.96 = 3.0$ times as bright
> What is the brightness ratio of Sirius, m = -1.48 and Adhera m = +1.48?
> (Ans: 15.3)

-the **absolute magnitude** is that seen from a distance of 10pc.
-if m is the apparent magnitude, d the distance in parsecs then the absolute magnitude M is given by the formula:

m - M = 5 log(d) - 5

-NB log here is log base 10, but appears as 'log' on a graphic calculator.
-to find d, rearrange to make log(d) the subject, then d will be '2nd' 'log' on the calculator (which is in fact the function 10^x).

> Worked example:
> Sirius has an apparent magnitude of −1.48 and is at a distance 2.6 parsec. What is the absolute magnitude?
> m = -1.48, d = 2.6pc
> m − M = 5 log d - 5
> -1.48 - M = 5 log 2.6 − 5
> M = -5 x 0.42 + 5 - 1.48 = +1.4.
> As the sun has an absolute magnitude of +4.8 then the luminosity of Sirius can be compared to the sun (4.8 - 1.4 = 3.4 magnitudes brighter or $2.511^{3.4}$ which is about 23 times as luminous as the sun.)
> Rigel is at 250pc and has an apparent magnitude of +0.1. Find the absolute magnitude and compare its luminosity to Sirius.
> (Ans: -6.9, 2100 times more luminous).

Spectroscopic parallax

Luminosity from spectrum

-the wavelength at peak intensity gives a star's surface temperature. This comes from Wien's law $T = 0.0029/\lambda_{max}$. See graph below left.

-the surface temperature gives spectral type.
-the darkness of the lines in the spectrum (and hence composition), help identify the star type (giant, supergiant etc). See middle graph below.
-this in turn gives absolute magnitude Mv. NB M is the same as Mv.
-knowing the apparent and absolute magnitude, a star's distance can be found using m - M = 5log(d)-5
-this method is called **spectroscopic parallax**.

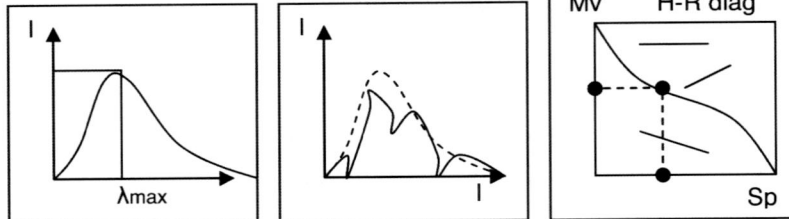

-as an example, suppose a star with an apparent magnitude of +3.5 is found from its spectrum to be type B7 and main sequence.
-look at your own HR diagram on page 11 and estimate the absolute magnitude of a B7 main sequence star.
-it is about -2.0. Using m = +3.5 and M = -2.0 then
Log(d) = (m-M+5)/5 = (3.5+2+5)/5 = 10.5/2 = 2.1 so d = 120 pc
-note there is a large error on Mv as all the star types cover a wide band and one estimates the Mv for the middle of the band.
Task-a star of m = +7.0 is known to be a white dwarf of type A5. Find the absolute mag and hence the distance.
Ans: an A5 white dwarf has an Mv of about +11.5 so log d = (7.0-11.5+5)/5
Log d = 0.7/2 = 0.35 so d = 2.4pc (NB this is Sirius' binary partner).

-alternatively, having found the luminosity L of the star from the spectrum and measuring the brightness b, the distance d can also be found using the formula

$$b = \frac{L}{4\pi d^2}$$

as an example, suppose the apparent brightness of a 61 Cyg is 3×10^{-7} W/m² and is found to have a luminosity of 2×10^{26} W, find the distance, in metres, ly and pc.
d² = L/4πb so =2×10^{26} /4π3 $\times 10^{-7}$ = 0.05 $\times 10^{th-32}$ 2.2 $\times 10^{16}$ = 2.5ly = 0.8pc

-this method is limited to distances less than 10Mpc.
-the spectral type of fainter stars is harder to determine.

Task box 3; time for a quick review. Fill in the missing key words in the spaces below, then check back. Good luck!

Task box 3
1. _____
2. _____
3. _____
4. _____
5. _____
6. _____
7. _____
8. _____
9. _____

(1) binary; a binary system detected by the Doppler shift of the lines in its spectrum. (2) diagram; a graph of the luminosity or magnitude of a star against its surface temperature or spectral type. (3); stars that are burning hydrogen by fusion. (4) :stars that are burning helium, and have expanded and cooled. (5); a star the size of the earth with no more fusion energy. (6); stars that are burning carbon and are large and luminous. (7); the distance of a star that has a parallax of one arc second. (8) magnitude; the magnitude of a star seen from 10pc. (9) parallax; determining the distance to a star using its spectral class.

16

Cepheid variables

-a **Cepheid** variable is a star that varies in brightness over a period of several days, due to changes in size and power output.
-they are named after the most famous one, Delta Cephei.
-a graph of the variation of magnitude against time for a star is called its **light curve.**

> Task. Plot the following points of the magnitude of Delta Cephei on the light curve graph below.

day	magnitude
0	3.4
1	3.6
2	3.8
3	4.0
4	4.2
5	3.8

6	3.4
7	3.6
8	3.8
9	4.0
10	4.2
11	3.8

Task box 3
Answers
1. spectroscopic.
2. Hertzsprung Russell.
3. main sequence.
4. red giant.
5. white dwarf.
6. supergiants.
7. parsec.
8. absolute.
9. spectroscopic.

Light curve for Delta Cephei

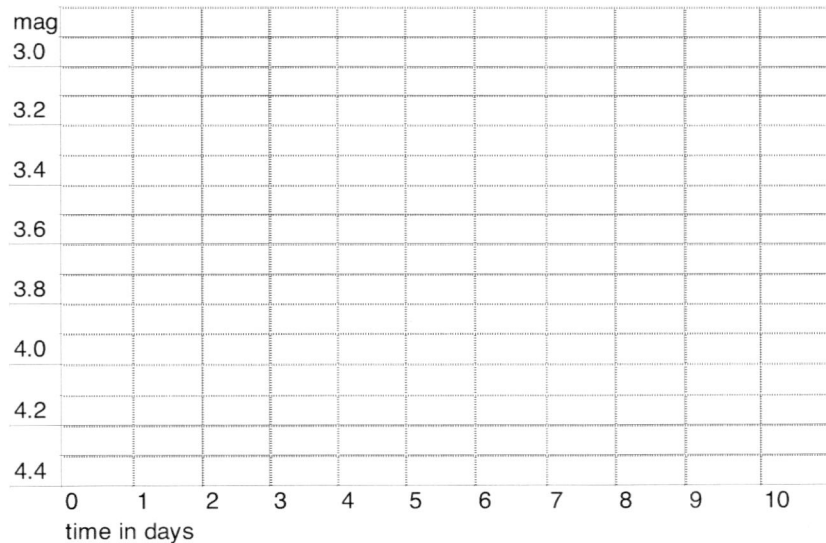

-Delta Cephei changes in brightness from about mag 3.4 to 4.2.
-this is a range of 0.8 mag or about a factor 2 in brightness.
-this repeats on a cycle of every five days or so.
-Cepheids are above the Main Sequence, spectral type around F/G.
-the period of variation increases with absolute magnitude.
-Cepheids are used for distance determination.
-the more luminous the Cepheid, the longer the period.
-the relationship is not linear and needs a special graph to illustrate the pattern as a straight line.

Cause of Cepheid Variability

Cepheids are passing through an instability phase. The cycle repeats over a regular period of days. A star that has enough helium, such as a giant that has left the main sequence, can undergo such oscillations. The cause for the cycle is shown in the flow chart below. NOTE, the yellow/orange colours of the boxes in the cycle reflect the colour changes of a cepheid as it varies.

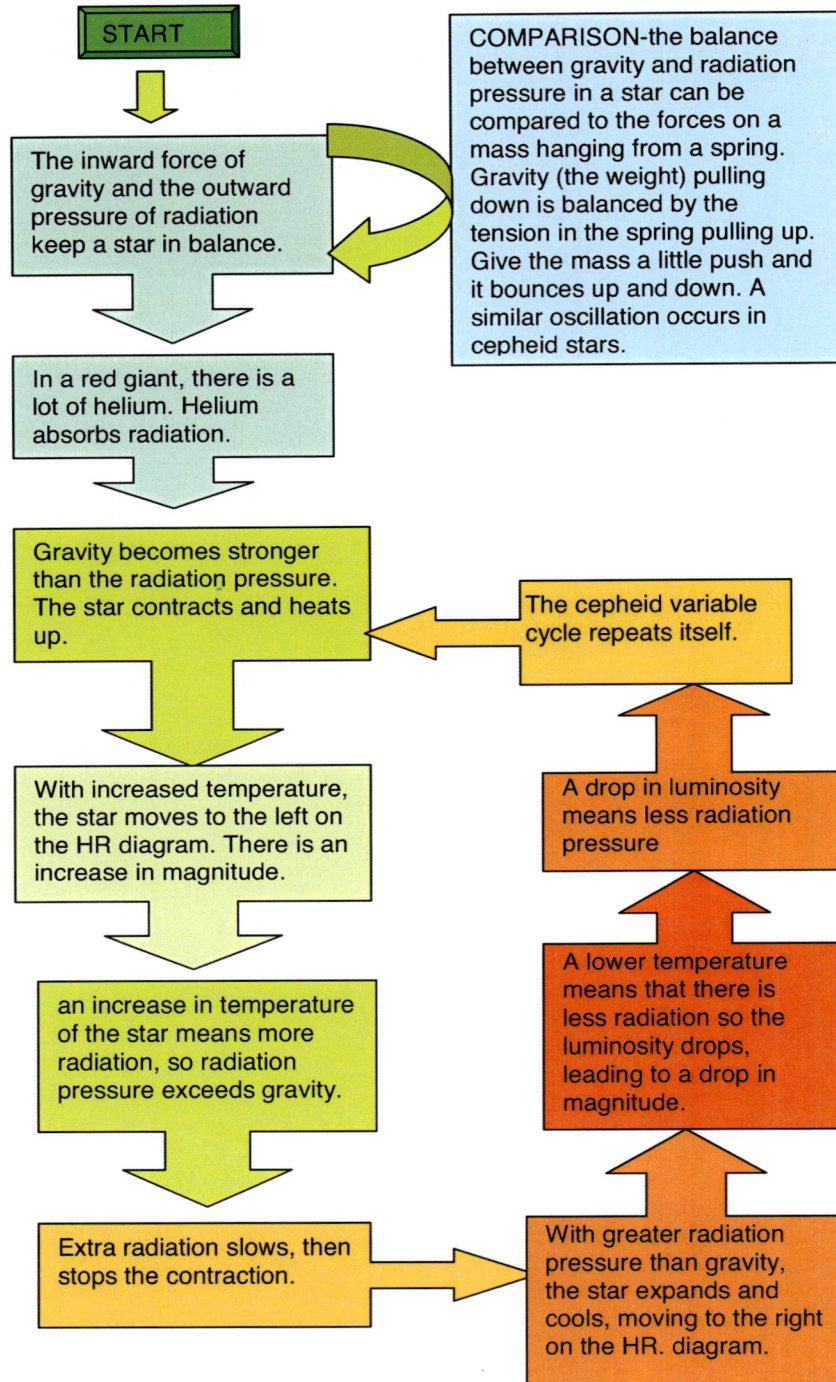

START

The inward force of gravity and the outward pressure of radiation keep a star in balance.

COMPARISON-the balance between gravity and radiation pressure in a star can be compared to the forces on a mass hanging from a spring. Gravity (the weight) pulling down is balanced by the tension in the spring pulling up. Give the mass a little push and it bounces up and down. A similar oscillation occurs in cepheid stars.

In a red giant, there is a lot of helium. Helium absorbs radiation.

Gravity becomes stronger than the radiation pressure. The star contracts and heats up.

The cepheid variable cycle repeats itself.

With increased temperature, the star moves to the left on the HR diagram. There is an increase in magnitude.

A drop in luminosity means less radiation pressure

an increase in temperature of the star means more radiation, so radiation pressure exceeds gravity.

A lower temperature means that there is less radiation so the luminosity drops, leading to a drop in magnitude.

Extra radiation slows, then stops the contraction.

With greater radiation pressure than gravity, the star expands and cools, moving to the right on the HR. diagram.

Task:
The cepheid variable cycle flow chart has been reproduced below, with
many of the key words missing. Fill in the blank spaces and then go back
and check them on the original diagram. Good luck!

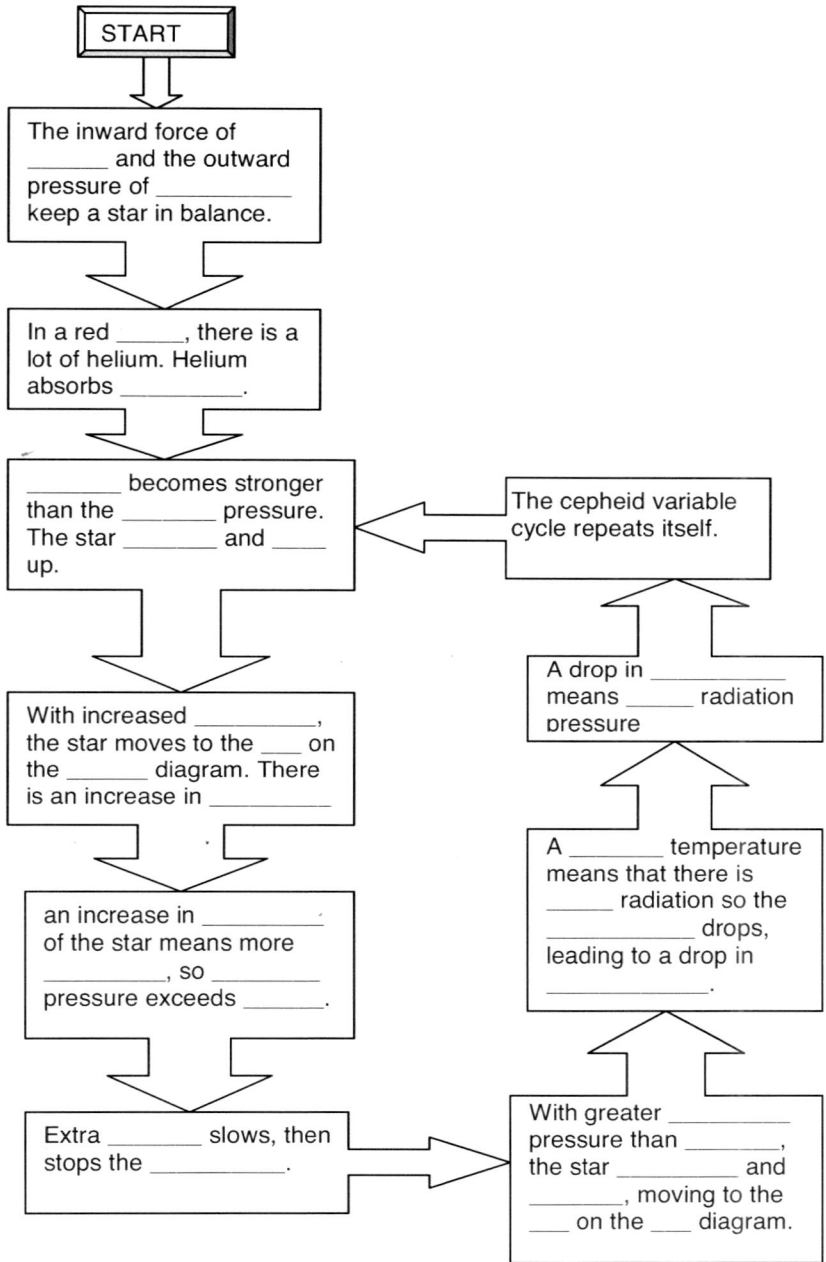

START

The inward force of
_____ and the outward
pressure of _____
keep a star in balance.

In a red _____, there is a
lot of helium. Helium
absorbs _____.

_____ becomes stronger
than the _____ pressure.
The star _____ and _____
up.

The cepheid variable
cycle repeats itself.

With increased _____,
the star moves to the ___ on
the _____ diagram. There
is an increase in _____

A drop in _____
means _____ radiation
pressure

an increase in _____
of the star means more
_____, so _____
pressure exceeds _____.

A _____ temperature
means that there is
_____ radiation so the
_____ drops,
leading to a drop in
_____.

Extra _____ slows, then
stops the _____.

With greater _____
pressure than _____,
the star _____ and
_____, moving to the
___ on the ___ diagram.

Task: a cepheid with a period of two days has an absolute magnitude of –2.5, while one with a period of 50 days has an absolute magnitude of –6.0. Plot these two points onto the blank log graph below and join them with a straight line.

Graph of period luminosity for cepheid variables

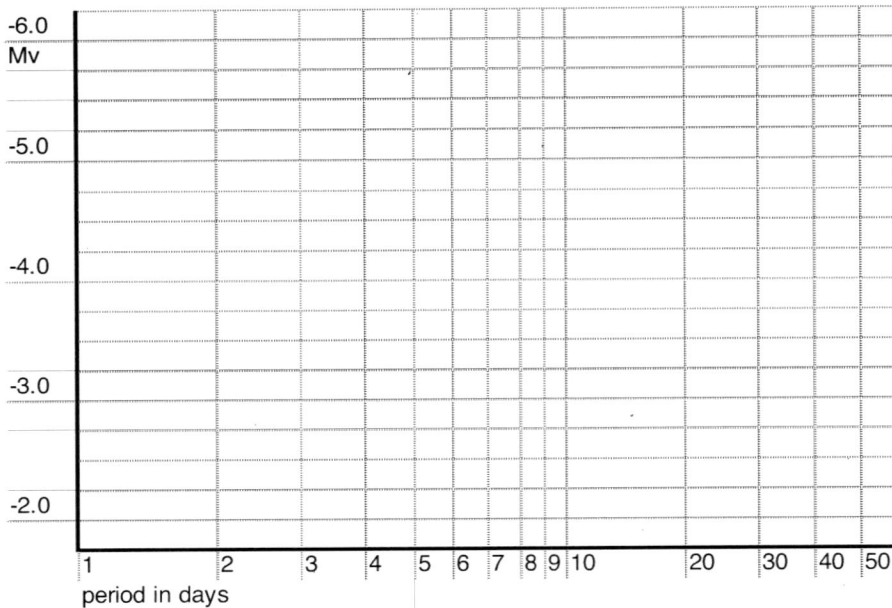

Worked example: Delta Cephi, has a period of five days and a mean apparent magnitude of +3.8. Find its absolute magnitude and distance.
Use period = 5 days, m = +3.8
Read off the graph, a period of 5 days gives M = -3.6
Use m-M = 5 log d-5
3.8 – ¯3.6 = 5 log d – 5, so log d = (3.8+3.6+5)/5 = 2.5 so d = 300pc.
Zeta Gem has a period of 10 days and an apparent magnitude of +4.0. Find the absolute magnitude and distance.
(Ans: -4.3, 460pc)

-a Cepheid in a nearby galaxy M31 has a mean magnitude of +21.5 and a period of 2.5 days. How far away is this galaxy?
Ans M = -2.8 so log d = (21.5+2.8 +5)/5 = 29.3/5 = 5.86 so d = 700 000 pc

Key points

-Cepheid variables are used as 'standard candles' for distance determination.
-the period luminosity law gives the absolute magnitude from the period, and with apparent magnitude the distance can be found.

Cosmology

Olber's Paradox

-Newton thought that the universe was infinite and static.

-if the universe was infinite, then in whichever direction we looked, we should see stars.
-if there was a star in every direction, then the night sky should look uniformly bright, the same brightness as the surface of the stars.
-the night sky is black, so this model of the universe must be wrong. This is known as **Olber's Paradox**.

-suppose that the universe was static and infinite.
-there would be the same density of stars in all parts of the universe.
-consider the stars found inside a spherical shell centred on the observer, distance d, thickness y and star density n.
-the number of stars in that shell will be;

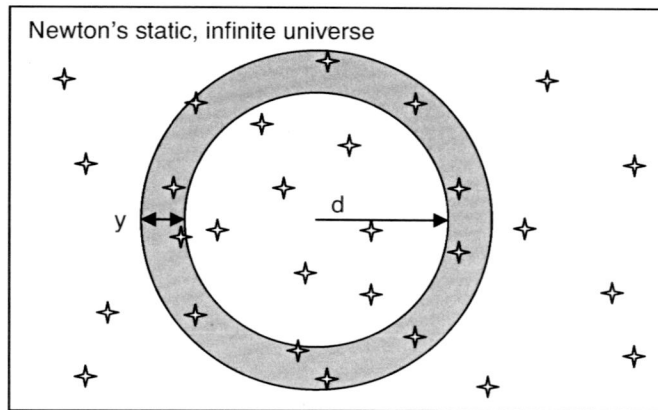

Newton's static, infinite universe

No. stars = volume x density

No. stars = area x thickness x density

$= 4.\pi.d^2.y.n$

Now the brightness of a star falls off inversely with the square of the distance via

$$b = \frac{L}{4\pi d^2}$$

so the total brightness of a shell of stars will be the product, giving

Lny.

-thus the brightness from a shell of stars is independent of distance.
-the more distant the shell, the fainter the stars look, but there are more stars in that shell and these two effects cancel out.
-each shell will add the same amount to the brightness of the sky and as there will be an infinite number of shells, the brightness of the sky will become infinite!

Total brightness = brightness from shell 1 + brightness from shell 2 + ...

Total brightness Σb = Lny + Lny + Lny + ... =

-obscuring material (eg dust) could cut out the light from the more distant stars. But the dust would heat up, until it glowed as brightly as the stars themselves, so it would still give a bright night sky.
-the night sky is black, so this model of the universe must be wrong

-Newton's law of gravity states that every piece of matter pulls on every other piece of matter.
-Objects would either be moving closer together due to gravity, or moving fast enough apart to escape the pull of gravity.
-the universe cannot be static.
-it must be finite and in motion.
-the Big Bang can help resolve this paradox.
-first, if the universe is finite, then there will not be an infinite number of stars, so the night sky will not be infinitely bright.
-the universe is expanding, so the light from the stars is red shifted to lower energies, reducing the brightness further.
-for stars too far away, their light has not yet reached us.

The Big Bang Model

Red Shift-The Doppler Effect

-when there is relative motion between a source of waves and an observer the frequency changes.
-this is called the **Doppler Effect**.
-if a star moves away from us, the wavefronts are created further apart compared to the star at rest.
-the wavelength is longer so the frequency is lower.
-the light is shifted to the red end of the spectrum-a **red shift**.
-if a star is approaching us, the wavefronts are created closer together, compared to the star at rest.
-the wavelength is shorter so the frequency is higher.
-the light is shifted to the blue end of the spectrum-a **blue shift**.
-rotation of a star or galaxy can be studied; one side will be approaching us (light is blue shifted) and the other side is moving away from us (red shifted).
-galaxies in our Local group show a mixture of blue and red shifts.
-this is because they are bound by gravity and on average some will be orbiting towards us and some orbiting away from us.
-outside the Local group, all other galaxies show a red shift.
-this means they are all moving away from us.
-the fainter ones (and therefore more distant) are moving away faster.
-if all galaxies are moving away from us, the further ones more rapidly, this suggests that the universe is expanding.
-if the universe is expanding, then at some time in the past, it occupied a much smaller volume, with an event like an explosion.
-this explosive start to the universe is called the **Big Bang** model.

Space time expansion

-time and space began with the universe in the Big Bang.
-objects are getting further apart and space itself is expanding.
-there is nothing outside the universe as space only exists within it.
-the universe is not expanding into an empty space, there is nothing outside space (not even a void!).
-time did not exist before the Big Bang.

Background radiation

-the temperature of a black body can be found from the peak in the curve as shown earlier using Wien's law.
-Penzias and Wilson found black body radiation coming from the universe. The **background radiation** peak is in the microwave part of the spectrum.
-the radiation is the same strength in all directions, (isotropic).
-Wein's law indicates a temperature of 3K
-the universe itself is behaving like a black body at 3K.

-as it is expanding, then it is cooling according to the Gas Laws.
-as an example, in a diesel engine, the gas is compressed suddenly in the cylinder so heats up enough to ignite the fuel.
-a CO^2 cylinder when the gas is allowed to rapidly escape and expand, cools down enough to become dry ice at -78°C.
-in the past, the universe was at a much higher temperature.

Development of the universe

-gravity is slowing down the expansion of the universe.
-the slowing depends on the density of the universe.
-enough mass and gravity could slow down the expansion and even reverse it. Such a universe is said to be **closed**.
-not enough matter and the universe would expand at a steady rate. Such a universe is said to be **open**.
-just the right amount of matter and the expansion rate would eventually be stopped. Such a universe is said to be **flat**.
-it appears that there is only 10% of the mass needed to stop the expansion, so the universe is open.
-there may still be mass that cannot be seen. **Brown dwarfs** are bodies not quite massive enough to start fusion and become stars.
-objects that no longer burn nuclear fusion are known as **black dwarfs** and could be distributed across the galaxy.

models of the universe

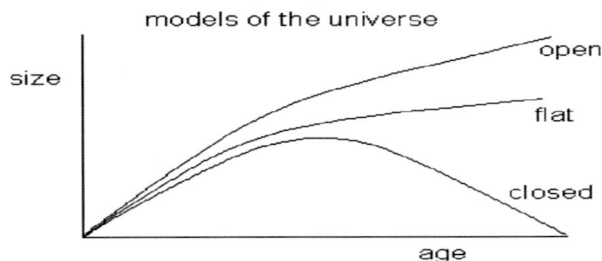

-brown and black dwarfs are called **MACHOS** (massive compact halo objects) and might account for the missing mass.
-missing mass could be in particles thought to be massless. They are known as **WIMPS** (weakly interacting massive particles).
-the **neutrino** is such a particle once believed to be massless but recently found to have a very small mass (1/17 millionth the electron mass!)
-this is far from being enough to close the universe!
-the mass that will stop the expansion of the universe with its present volume is called the **critical density**.
-if the density is greater than this then it will slow down the expansion, stop, then collapse and therefore become a closed universe.
-if the density is below critical, the universe will expand forever and become open.
-if it has exactly the critical value, then the universe will be flat and the expansion will be stopped (though it will take forever!).
-current scientific evidence suggests that there is not enough mass to stop the expansion of the universe and therefore it is open.

```
Task box 4 : fill in the blank spaces below, then check your answers.
You shouldn't need luck by now!
```

(1): a star that varies in brightness on a regular cycle. (2): a graph showing how a star's brightness changes with time. (3): a star used to find the distance to other stars.(4): the paradox indicating how dark the sky should be.(5): the change in frequency of a source of waves when there is motion between the source and observer. (6): the increase in wavelength from a receding source of light. (7): the decrease in wavelength from an approaching light source (8): the model of the universe that starts with an explosion. (9): the radiation left over from the cooling down of the universe after the initial explosion. (10): a universe where the expansion continues indefinitely. (11): a universe where the expansion will eventually stop. (12): a universe which will eventually contract. (13): MACHOs (14): an object no longer fusion burning. (15): a body that isn't hot enough for fusion burning. (16): an almost massless particle. (17): WIMPs. (18): the density that will stop the expansion of the universe.

Task box 4
1. _____
2. _____
   _____
3. _____
   _____
4. _____
5. _____
   _____
6. _____
7. _____
8. _____
   _____
9. _____
10. _____
11. _____
12. _____
13. _____
   _____
   _____
   _____
14. _____
   _____
15. _____
   _____
16. _____
17. _____
   _____
   _____
   _____
18. _____

International Research

-the IB expects students to be familiar with at least one example of an international astrophysics project.
-one has been given below, but many can be found in great detail on the internet.

Example of international research

Project Herschel

-the Centre National d'Etudes Spatiales CNES is the agency responsible for France's space policy in Europe.
-CNES is working with ESA the European Space Agency and NASA.
-Herschel is a space observatory that will be launched in June 2008 by ESA's Arianne 5 rocket and should run for three years.
-it contains a 3.5m telescope, the largest to date to be put in space.
-it will be able to study the complete spectrum from microwaves to sub mm.
-the aim is to study the 'cold' objects such as the interstellar medium, star formation areas and the oldest 'primordial' galaxies.
-it will be able to detect the molecular content and see if those important to life exist elsewhere.

The value of such research

-specific values can be given for any one international astrophysics project selected.
-there are some general advantages that will cover most examples:

-international projects allow the cost of an expensive programme to be shared between the co operating countries, where individually they could not afford it.
-international cooperation in such projects brings countries closer together are reduce the likelihood of war.
-many of the projects that are looking out at the universe have direct applications for studying and hence sustaining life on earth.
-the knowledge gained by such projects leads to a better understanding of the universe and the part the human race plays.

Task box 4
Answers
1. Cepheid.
2. light curve.
3. standard candle.
4. Olbers.
5. Doppler Effect.
6. redshift.
7. blueshift.
8. big bang.
9. microwave
(background).
10. open.
11. flat.
12. closed.
13. massive
compact halo object.
14. black dwarf.
15. brown dwarf.
16. neutrino.
17. weakly
interacting massive
particles.
18. critical.

High Level Extension

Stellar processes and evolution

Formation of stars

The evolution of a star depends on its mass. The main stages are shown in the flow chart below. NOTE mass given here is in terms of the solar mass (1M) and masses for the limits at each stage are after any mass loss.

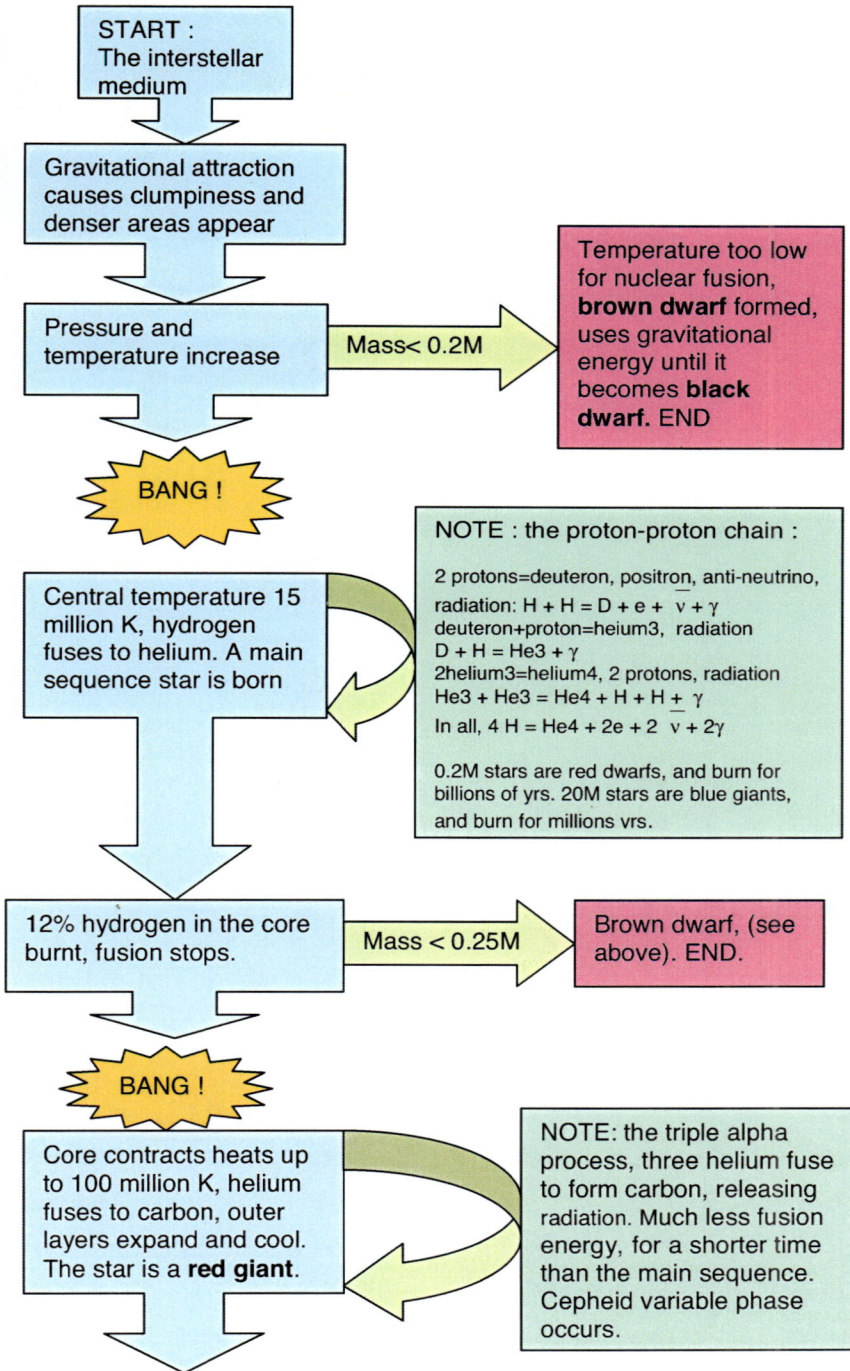

START :
The interstellar medium

Gravitational attraction causes clumpiness and denser areas appear

Pressure and temperature increase

Mass< 0.2M

Temperature too low for nuclear fusion, **brown dwarf** formed, uses gravitational energy until it becomes **black dwarf.** END

BANG !

Central temperature 15 million K, hydrogen fuses to helium. A main sequence star is born

NOTE : the proton-proton chain :

2 protons=deuteron, positron, anti-neutrino, radiation: $H + H = D + e + \bar{\nu} + \gamma$
deuteron+proton=heium3, radiation
$D + H = He3 + \gamma$
2helium3=helium4, 2 protons, radiation
$He3 + He3 = He4 + H + H + \gamma$
In all, $4 H = He4 + 2e + 2 \bar{\nu} + 2\gamma$

0.2M stars are red dwarfs, and burn for billions of yrs. 20M stars are blue giants, and burn for millions yrs.

12% hydrogen in the core burnt, fusion stops.

Mass < 0.25M

Brown dwarf, (see above). END.

BANG !

Core contracts heats up to 100 million K, helium fuses to carbon, outer layers expand and cool. The star is a **red giant**.

NOTE: the triple alpha process, three helium fuse to form carbon, releasing radiation. Much less fusion energy, for a shorter time than the main sequence. Cepheid variable phase occurs.

Helium used in core, fusion stops

Mass < 1.4M

NOTE-this mass is the **Chandrasekhar limit**

BANG !

NOVA !

Core contracts, heats up to 1000 million K, carbon fusing to silicon starts. The star is a **supergiant**.

Star collapses, outer layers thrown off forming a **planetary nebula**, brightening by 10 magnitudes to become **nova**.

Fusion burning in core reaches iron, then stops. Sudden reversal turns iron back to helium releasing much energy.

Star earth size, electrons forced into lowest orbits, degenerate matter, gravitational energy becoming radiation, heats up. Star is a **white dwarf**.

SUPER NOVA !

Star cools to brown then black dwarf when energy runs out. END.

Outer layers ejected at high speed, elements heavier than iron created, enriching the interstellar medium, star brightens by 20 magnitudes, taking years to fade.

Mass<2.5M

Core collapses to a few km across, electrons join with protons in atoms to make neutrons. Neutron pressure stops further collapse. A **neutron star** is formed.

Mass > 2.5M the **Oppenheimer-Volkof** limit

A neutron star's strong magnetic field gives out radiation from the poles, seen as flashes as it spins. It is a **pulsar**.

Core contracts, neutron pressure not enough to stop collapse to zero volume. Escape velocity greater than the speed of light. **A black hole** is formed. Matter falling in gives out X-rays. END.

Neutron star/pulsar cools down as it loses only remaining energy (heat). END.

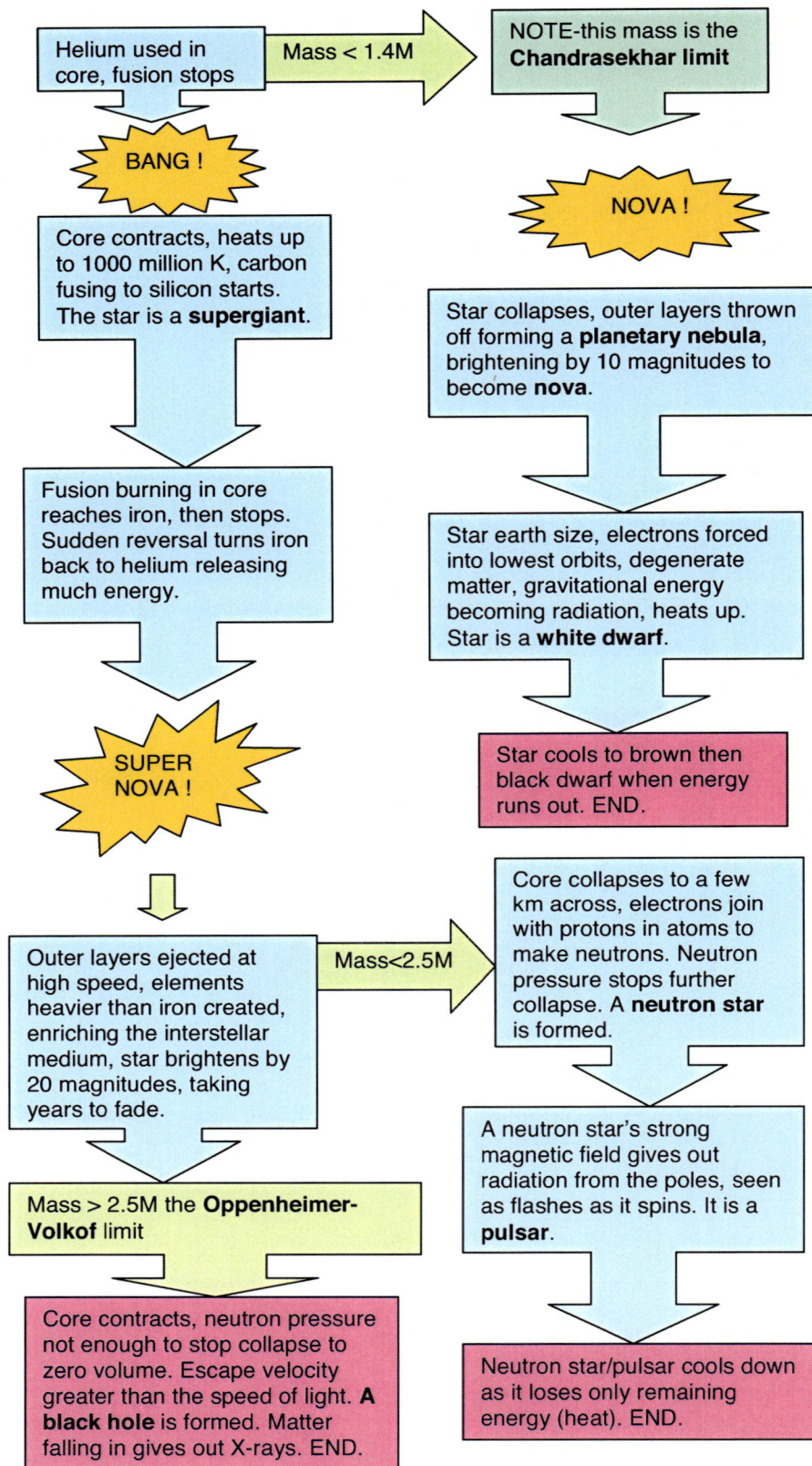

Task : the stellar evolution flow chart has been drawn again, with keys words removed. Fill in the blank spaces, then check back with the original. Good luck!

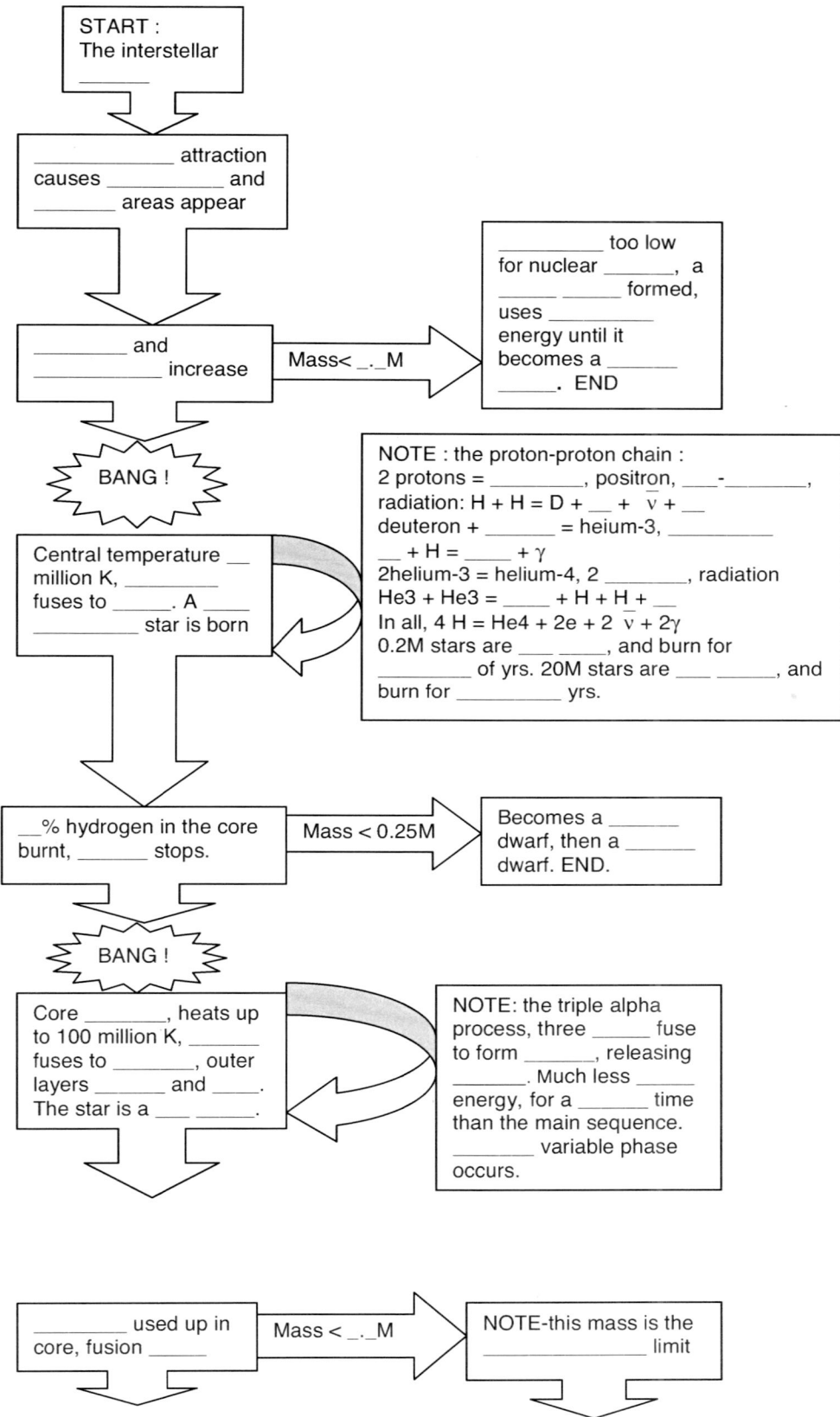

START :
The interstellar _____

_____ attraction causes _____ and _____ areas appear

_____ and _____ increase

Mass< _._M →

_____ too low for nuclear _____, a _____ _____ formed, uses _____ energy until it becomes a _____ _____. END

BANG !

Central temperature __ million K, _____ fuses to _____. A ____ _____ star is born

NOTE : the proton-proton chain :
2 protons = _____, positron, ___-_____, radiation: H + H = D + __ + $\bar{\nu}$ + __
deuteron + _____ = heium-3, _____
__ + H = ____ + γ
2helium-3 = helium-4, 2 _____, radiation
He3 + He3 = ____ + H + H + __
In all, 4 H = He4 + 2e + 2 $\bar{\nu}$ + 2γ
0.2M stars are ___ ____, and burn for _____ of yrs. 20M stars are ___ ____, and burn for _____ yrs.

__% hydrogen in the core burnt, _____ stops.

Mass < 0.25M →

Becomes a _____ dwarf, then a _____ dwarf. END.

BANG !

Core _____, heats up to 100 million K, _____ fuses to _____, outer layers _____ and ____. The star is a ___ ____.

NOTE: the triple alpha process, three ____ fuse to form _____, releasing _____. Much less ____ energy, for a _____ time than the main sequence. _____ variable phase occurs.

_____ used up in core, fusion _____

Mass < _._M →

NOTE-this mass is the _____ limit

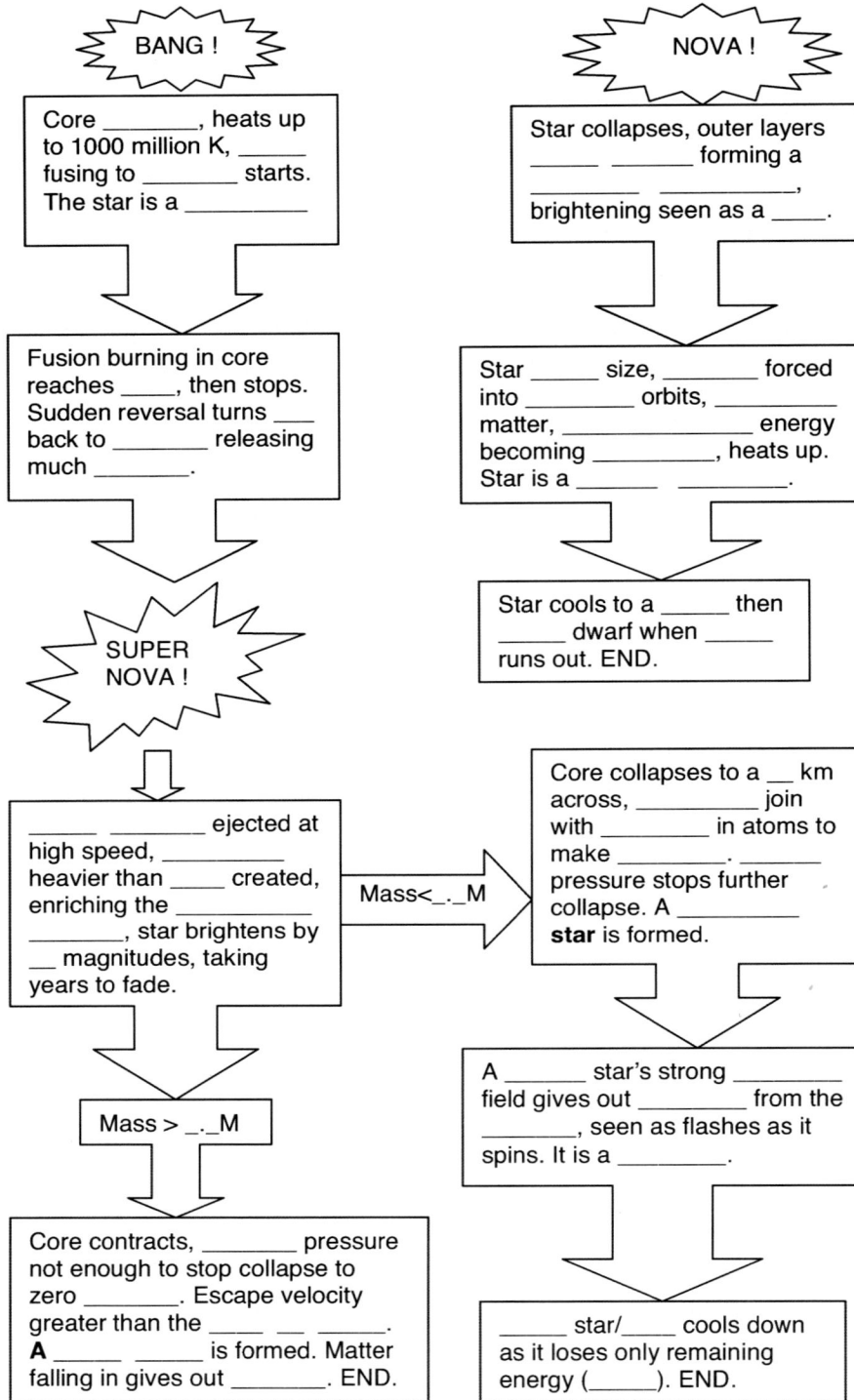

BANG !

Core _____, heats up to 1000 million K, _____ fusing to _____ starts. The star is a _____

NOVA !

Star collapses, outer layers _____ _____ forming a _____ _____, brightening seen as a ____.

Fusion burning in core reaches ____, then stops. Sudden reversal turns ___ back to _____ releasing much _____.

Star _____ size, _____ forced into _____ orbits, _____ matter, _____ energy becoming _____, heats up. Star is a _____ _____.

Star cools to a _____ then _____ dwarf when _____ runs out. END.

SUPER NOVA !

_____ _____ ejected at high speed, _____ heavier than ____ created, enriching the _____ _____, star brightens by __ magnitudes, taking years to fade.

Mass<_._M

Core collapses to a __ km across, _____ join with _____ in atoms to make _____. _____ pressure stops further collapse. A _____ **star** is formed.

Mass > _._M

A _____ star's strong _____ field gives out _____ from the _____, seen as flashes as it spins. It is a _____.

Core contracts, _____ pressure not enough to stop collapse to zero _____. Escape velocity greater than the ____ __ _____. A _____ _____ is formed. Matter falling in gives out _____. END.

_____ star/____ cools down as it loses only remaining energy (_____). END.

28

Mass Luminosity Relation

Name of star	Mv	mass M sun = 1	log M
Sun	+4.8	1.0	
Eta Cas A	+4.6	0.85	
Eta Cas B	+8.7	0.52	
UV Cet	+15.8	0.035	
o² Cet	+6.0	0.8	
C	+12.7	0.21	
Sirius	+1.4	2.3	
Procyon	+2.7	1.8	

Task : calculate the log of the stars' masses and complete the table to 2dp. Then plot the points on the graph shown below. What kind of relationship is there between the mass of a star and its absolute magnitude? And hence luminosity?

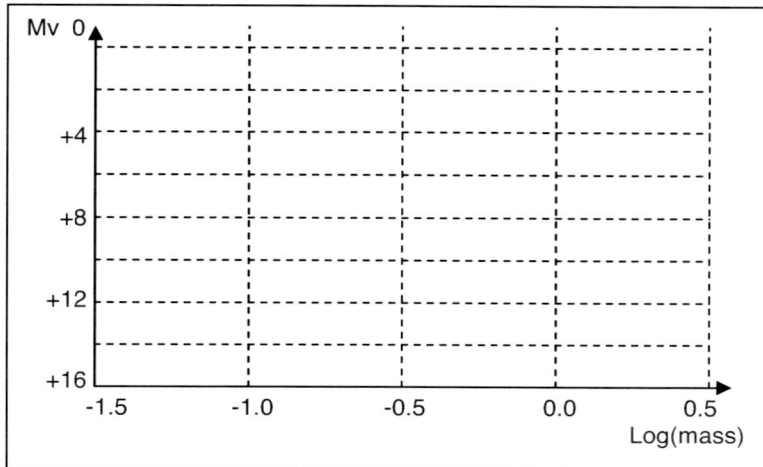

-the luminosity of a star depends on its mass.
-there is a simple relationship between the two.
-If L is the star's luminosity compared to the sun and M is the mass in terms of the solar mass then

$$\log L = 3.45 \log M$$

Putting it another way

$$L = M^{3.45}$$

-so for a star twice the mass of the sun, it will have a luminosity $2^{3.45}$ or about 11 times as luminous (this is about 2.6 magnitudes).
-a star that is 20 times the mass of the sun will be $20^{3.45}$ as luminous or about 30800 times as bright (about 11.2 magnitudes)

Pulsars

-a pulsar is a very fast spinning neutron star.

Neutron star

-if a star is between 1.4 and 2.5 solar masses, it evolves into a neutron star.
-after the supernova explosion all the electrons are pushed into the nuclei.
-this turns all the protons into neutrons.
-the density of a neutron star is a thousand billion times that of water.
-it is only a few km across!

-due to conservation of angular momentum, as a star shrinks in size, it spins faster (think of the spinning ice skater pulling in her arms).
-a neutron star could be taking only milliseconds to rotate once on its axis.
-they have very strong magnetic fields, whose poles don't quite match up with their geographic poles.
-charged particles falling into their fields at the poles release radiation.
-(the aurora borealis or northern lights on the earth form in a similar way).
-these flashes are seen every time the neutron star spins, if we lie in the beam (much like the beam of light from a lighthouse).
-a neutron star that is seen to flash is called a pulsar.
-such a star has been detected in the Crab Nebula, the remains of a supernova explosion seen in 1054.

Galaxies and the expanding universe

Galactic motion

Milky Way

-the galaxy in which the solar system is situated is called **the Milky Way**.
-the Milky Way is a member of the Local Group of galaxies.
-it is a spiral galaxy, having a central bulge of many closely packed stars, gas and dust with a massive black hole in the centre.
-outside this is a flat disc of stars, dust and gas, in a spiral arm formation.
-the Milky Way is about 30kpc across, the solar system 10pc from the centre.
-It is enveloped in a spherical volume of material known as the **halo**. It is very tenuous, containing some very old stars and peculiar ones with very eccentric orbits, and other matter (see earlier for missing mass).

Types of galaxies

-**spiral galaxies** are disc shaped collections of stars, dust and gas. They have a central bulge, a tenuous halo and most material in spiral arms.
-**elliptical galaxies** are spheroidal collections of stars, dust and gas, more compact towards the centre, from perfectly spherical, to very elliptical.
-**irregular galaxies** show no regular shape at all.

Galactic distribution

-a **galactic cluster** is a group of galaxies gravitationally bound together and orbit round a common centre of gravity.
-larger groupings of galactic clusters are called **superclusters**.
-the Local Group is a 'satellite' cluster of the large Virgo supercluster.

Red shift of galaxies

When light sources are moving away from us, the light is shifted to the red end of the spectrum. This example of the Doppler Effect is called the red shift. Light sources approaching us show a blue shift. The shifting of light to the blue end or the red end of the spectrum is seen with galaxies, both in connection with their rotation rates and their velocities towards or away from us.

Task box 5: fill in the blank spaces below, then check back over the high level extension.

(1); an object with not enough mass to use fusion energy. (2); an object that has no fusion nor gravitational energy. (3); a star that has started helium burning to carbon, has expanded and cooled. (4); a star that has started carbon burning to silicon. (5): a star a few km across made of neutrons. (6); a spinning neutron star. (7); the brightening of a star by ten magnitudes when it expels its outer layers. (8); the resulting gas cloud from a nova. (9); the destruction of a star in a massive explosion.(10); an object whose escape velocity is greater than that of light. (11); the galaxy in which the sun is found. (12); the sparse material that surrounds our galaxy. (13); a disc-shaped galaxy with a central bulge and curved arms. (14); a spherical shaped galaxy. (15); a galaxy with no shape. (16) limit; the limit of 1.4 solar masses that determines whether a star becomes a white dwarf or neutron star. (17); a group of galaxies bound by gravity. (18); a large collection of galactic clusters.

Task box 5
1._____
2._____
3._____
4._____
5._____
6._____
7._____
8._____
9._____
10._____
11._____
12._____
13._____
14._____
15._____
16._____
17._____
18. _____

Red shift equation

-hydrogen is found everywhere in the universe.
-the wavelengths of the lines in the hydrogen spectrum are known.
-changes in their positions can be easily detected.
-the positions of the lines in a spectrum can be measured and then compared to the known wavelengths.
-if the lines show a blue shift, the object is approaching us.
-if they show a red shift then the object is moving away.

If the velocity of the light source is v and the speed of light is c, the original wavelength is λ and the change in wavelength $\Delta\lambda$ then they are related via;

velocity of source/velocity of light = wavelength change/wavelength

$$\frac{v}{c} = \frac{\Delta\lambda}{\lambda}$$

Worked example
If the hydrogen line of 650nm in the lab is found to be 683nm from a particular galaxy, the galaxy is moving away from us at;

v/c = (683-650)/650 (speed of light being 300 000kms^{-1}).
v = 15 000kms^{-1} .
If the hydrogen line was shifted to 637nm, find the velocity
(Ans: –6000kms^{-1}, the negative sign showing the galaxy is approaching us).

Note, this equation applies to velocities well below the speed of light and therefore ignores relativity.

Hubble's law

-for similar types of galaxies, fainter ones are further away.

-Hubble measured the Doppler Shift in galactic spectra.
-Hubble noticed that the fainter (more distant) galaxies had a greater red shift than the brighter (nearby) galaxies.
-the more distant galaxies are moving away from us at a faster rate.
-Hubble found a linear relationship between the recessional velocity of a galaxy and its distance. This is known as **Hubble's Law**.

-the Milky Way belongs to the Local Group of galaxies.
-the two dozen galaxies orbit about their common centre of gravity.
-half show a blue shift, half show a red shift, due to their random motions.
-outside the Local Group, every cluster of galaxies shows a red shift. -all galactic clusters are moving away from us.

If v is the recessional velocity in km/s and d is the distance n megaparsecs Mpc, then Hubble's law states

v = Hd

Where H is the **Hubble constant**.

Task
A galaxy that is moving 200kms^{-1} away from us is 4Mpc away. Take this information and plot it onto the graph shown below. Join this point to the origin with a straight line.

Graph of Hubble's Law

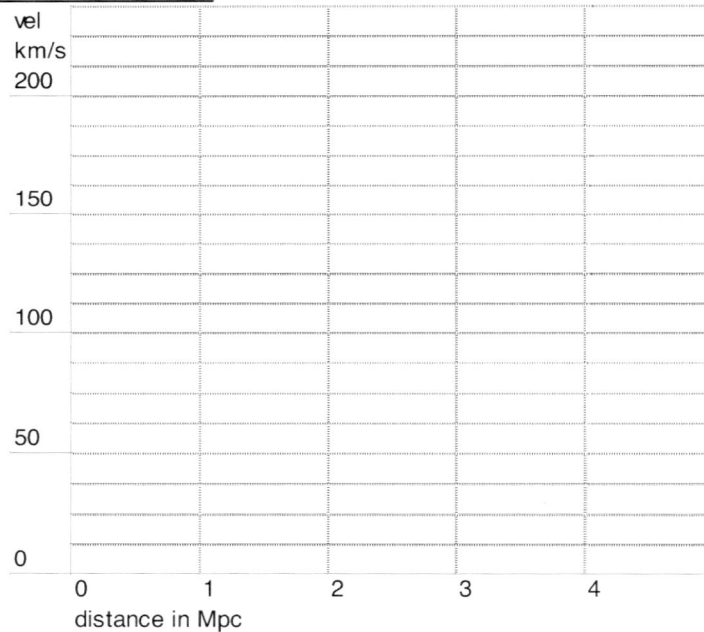

Task box 5
answers
1. brown dwarf.
2. black dwarf.
3. red giant.
4. supergiant.
5. neutron.
6. pulsar.
7. nova.
8. planetary nebula.
9. supernova.
10. black hole.
11. milky way.
12. halo.
13. spiral.
14. oval.
15. irregular.
16.Chandrasekhar.
17.galactic cluster.
18. supercluster.

Worked example: Suppose a galaxy has a recessional velocity of 125km/s. The graph can be used to find out how far away it is.
Draw a line from 125kms^{-1} across the graph to the line and continue it down to the distance axis. The distance given is 2.5Mpc.
A galaxy is 1.5Mpc away. What is its red shift velocity?
(Ans: 75kms^{-1})

As v = Hd, the gradient gives you the Hubble constant.

> Task: Measure the gradient of the graph. Don't forget units!

The value of the Hubble constant is about H = 50 kms^{-1}Mpc^{-1}. This means that the recessional velocity of a galaxy increases by 50kms^{-1} for every Megaparsec it is away from us.

The age of universe

-the more distant galaxies are moving faster away from us.
  -everything was once closer together, so the universe must be expanding.
-if the expansion rate is constant, one can find when the universe was created, the distance between galaxies being zero.

Worked example. Taking the Hubble constant to be 50kms^{-1}Mpc^{-1}, how long would it take to travel 1Mpc at a speed of 50kms^{-1}?
50km/s = 5 x 10^4 ms^{-1}. This is the velocity v.
1Mpc is 3.26 x 10^6 light years (1pc = 3.26ly)
A light year is 9.5 x 10^{15}m, so 1Mpc is 3 x 10^{22} m. This is the distance x.
As velocity = distance/time, then time = distance/velocity, t = x/v
t = 3 x 10^{22} / 5 x 10^4 which is 6 x 10^{17} sec, or about 20 billion years.
If the oldest object so far seen (13 billion yrs) was created at the beginning of the universe, what would be Hubble's constant?
(Ans: 77Kms^{-1}Mpc^{-1} 2sf)

The Universe-Time Line

The evolution of the universe is shown in the flow chart below

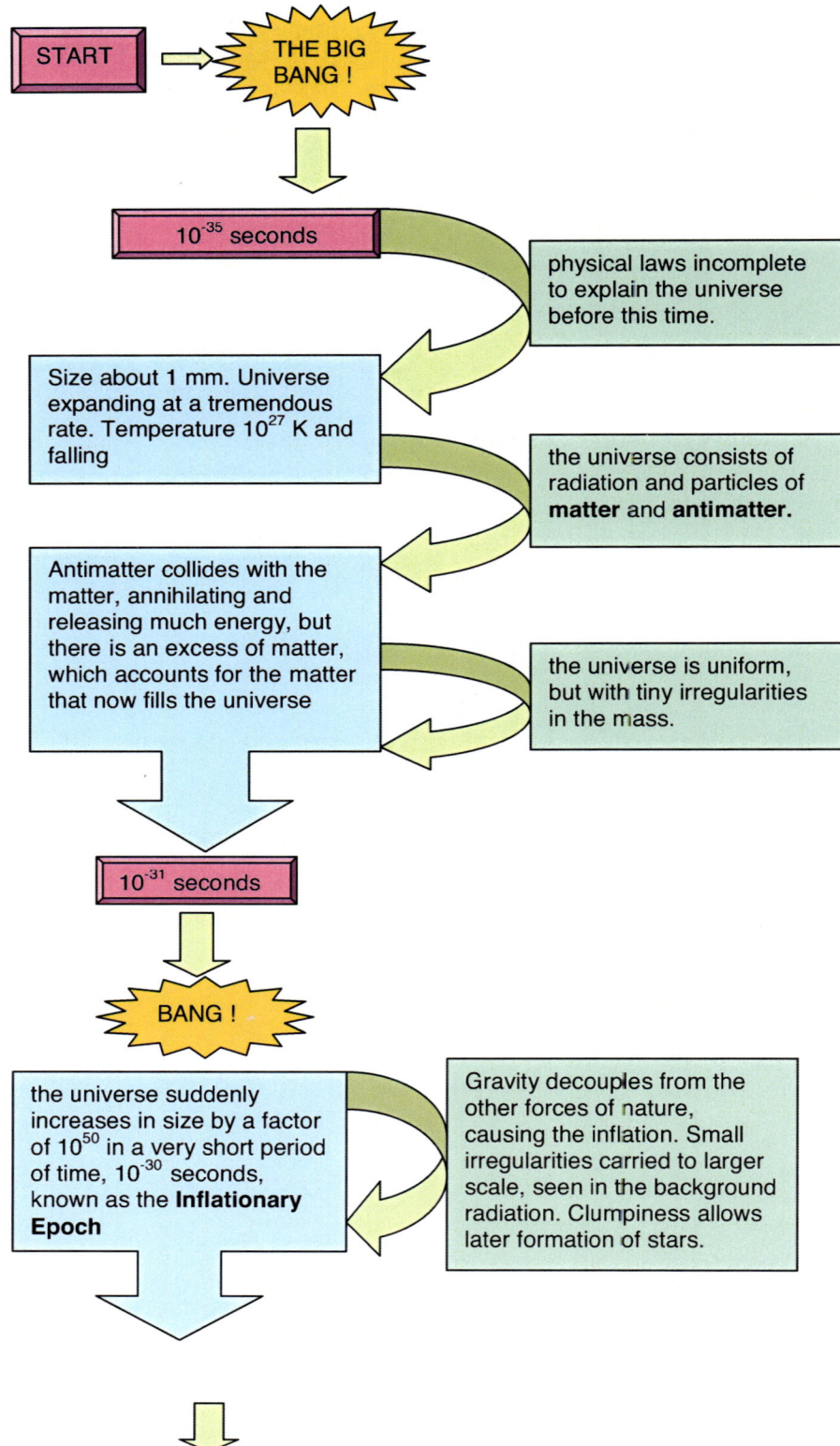

START → THE BIG BANG !

10^{-35} seconds

physical laws incomplete to explain the universe before this time.

Size about 1 mm. Universe expanding at a tremendous rate. Temperature 10^{27} K and falling

the universe consists of radiation and particles of **matter** and **antimatter.**

Antimatter collides with the matter, annihilating and releasing much energy, but there is an excess of matter, which accounts for the matter that now fills the universe

the universe is uniform, but with tiny irregularities in the mass.

10^{-31} seconds

BANG !

the universe suddenly increases in size by a factor of 10^{50} in a very short period of time, 10^{-30} seconds, known as the **Inflationary Epoch**

Gravity decouples from the other forces of nature, causing the inflation. Small irregularities carried to larger scale, seen in the background radiation. Clumpiness allows later formation of stars.

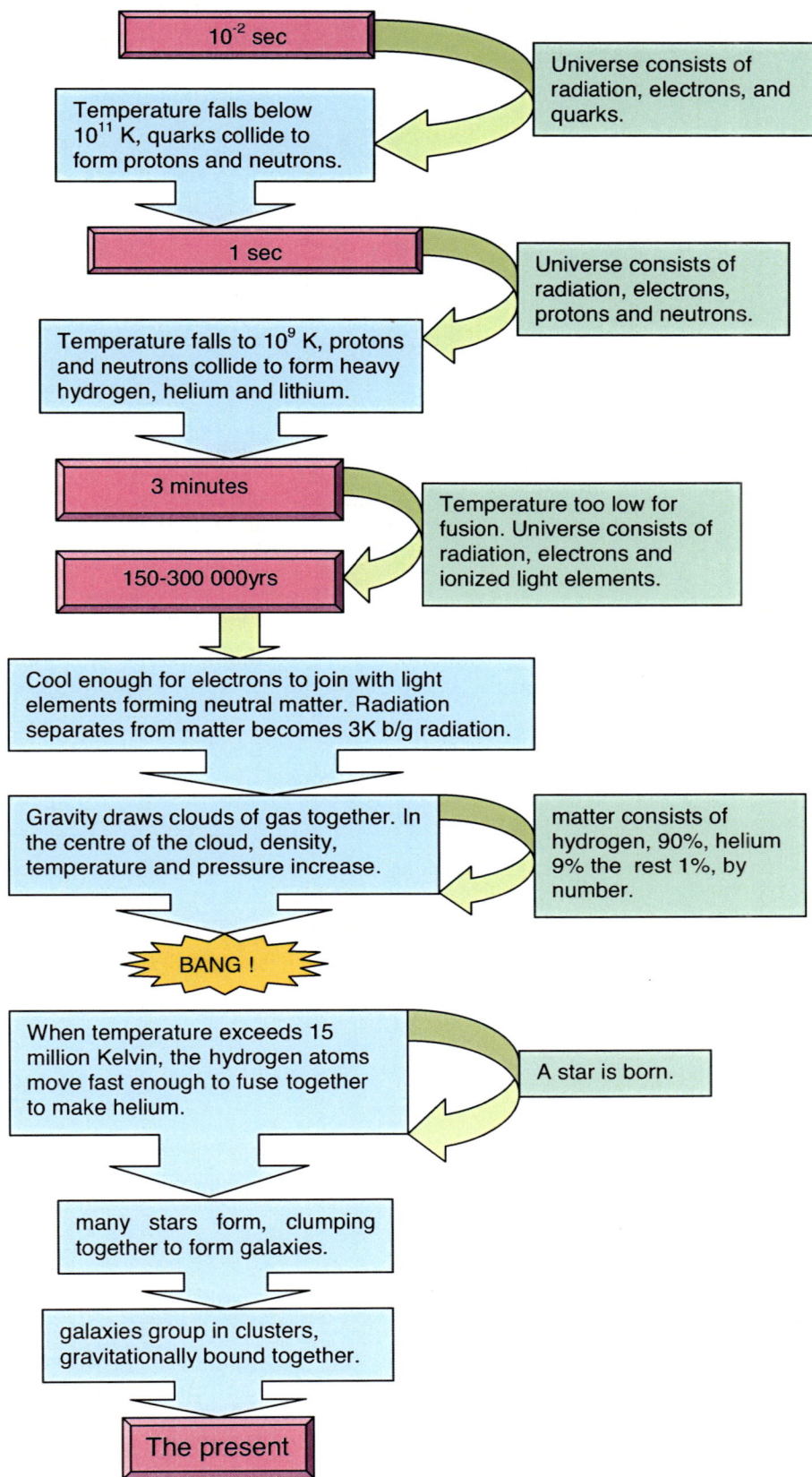

10^{-2} sec

Universe consists of radiation, electrons, and quarks.

Temperature falls below 10^{11} K, quarks collide to form protons and neutrons.

1 sec

Universe consists of radiation, electrons, protons and neutrons.

Temperature falls to 10^9 K, protons and neutrons collide to form heavy hydrogen, helium and lithium.

3 minutes

Temperature too low for fusion. Universe consists of radiation, electrons and ionized light elements.

150-300 000yrs

Cool enough for electrons to join with light elements forming neutral matter. Radiation separates from matter becomes 3K b/g radiation.

Gravity draws clouds of gas together. In the centre of the cloud, density, temperature and pressure increase.

matter consists of hydrogen, 90%, helium 9% the rest 1%, by number.

BANG !

When temperature exceeds 15 million Kelvin, the hydrogen atoms move fast enough to fuse together to make helium.

A star is born.

many stars form, clumping together to form galaxies.

galaxies group in clusters, gravitationally bound together.

The present

Universe Time Line Revision

Task : fill in the missing words in the flow chart below, then check your answers with the original. Good luck !

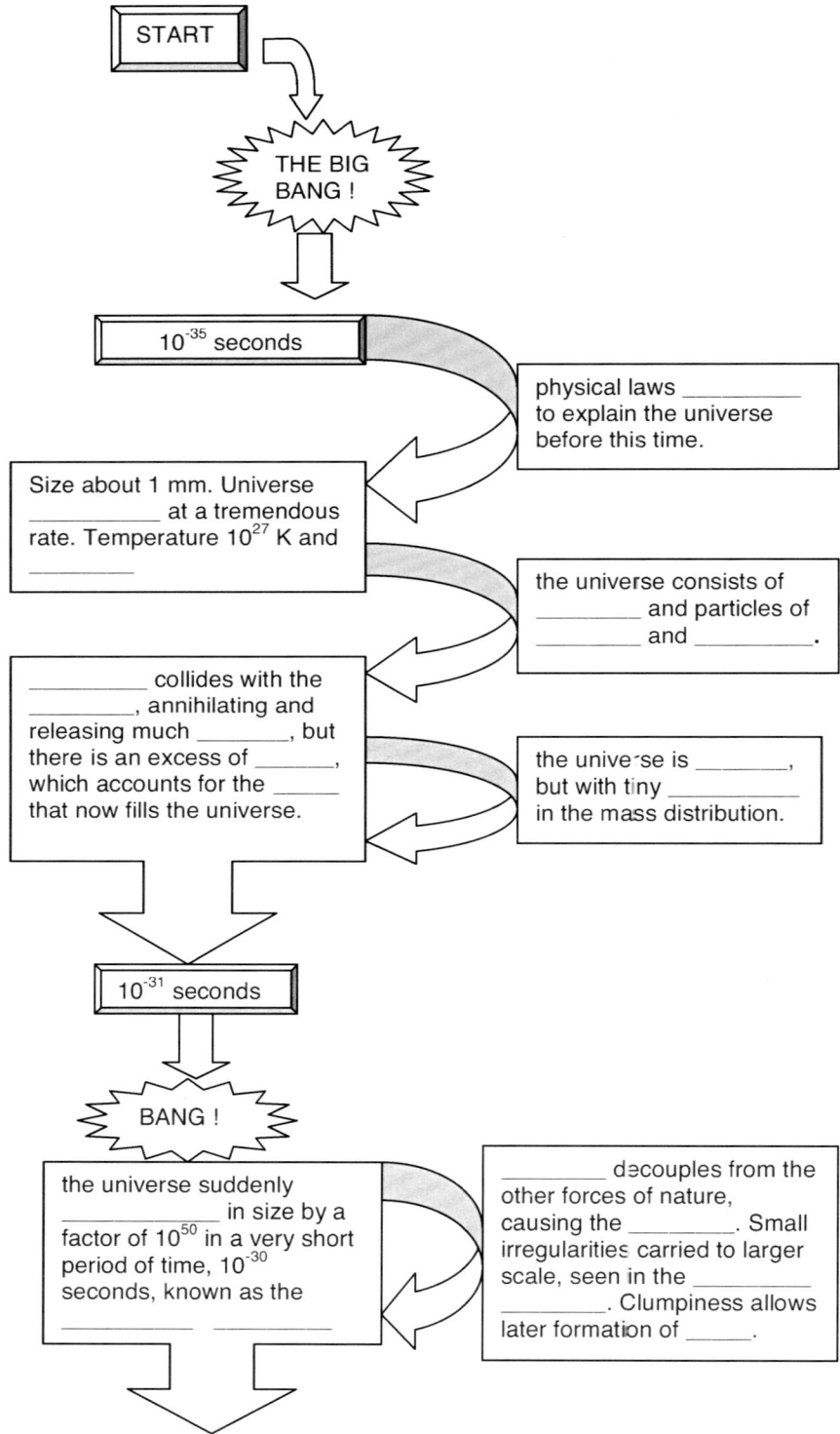

START

THE BIG BANG !

10^{-35} seconds

physical laws _____ to explain the universe before this time.

Size about 1 mm. Universe _____ at a tremendous rate. Temperature 10^{27} K and _____

the universe consists of _____ and particles of _____ and _____.

_____ collides with the _____, annihilating and releasing much _____, but there is an excess of _____, which accounts for the _____ that now fills the universe.

the universe is _____, but with tiny _____ in the mass distribution.

10^{-31} seconds

BANG !

the universe suddenly _____ in size by a factor of 10^{50} in a very short period of time, 10^{-30} seconds, known as the _____ _____

_____ decouples from the other forces of nature, causing the _____. Small irregularities carried to larger scale, seen in the _____ _____. Clumpiness allows later formation of _____.

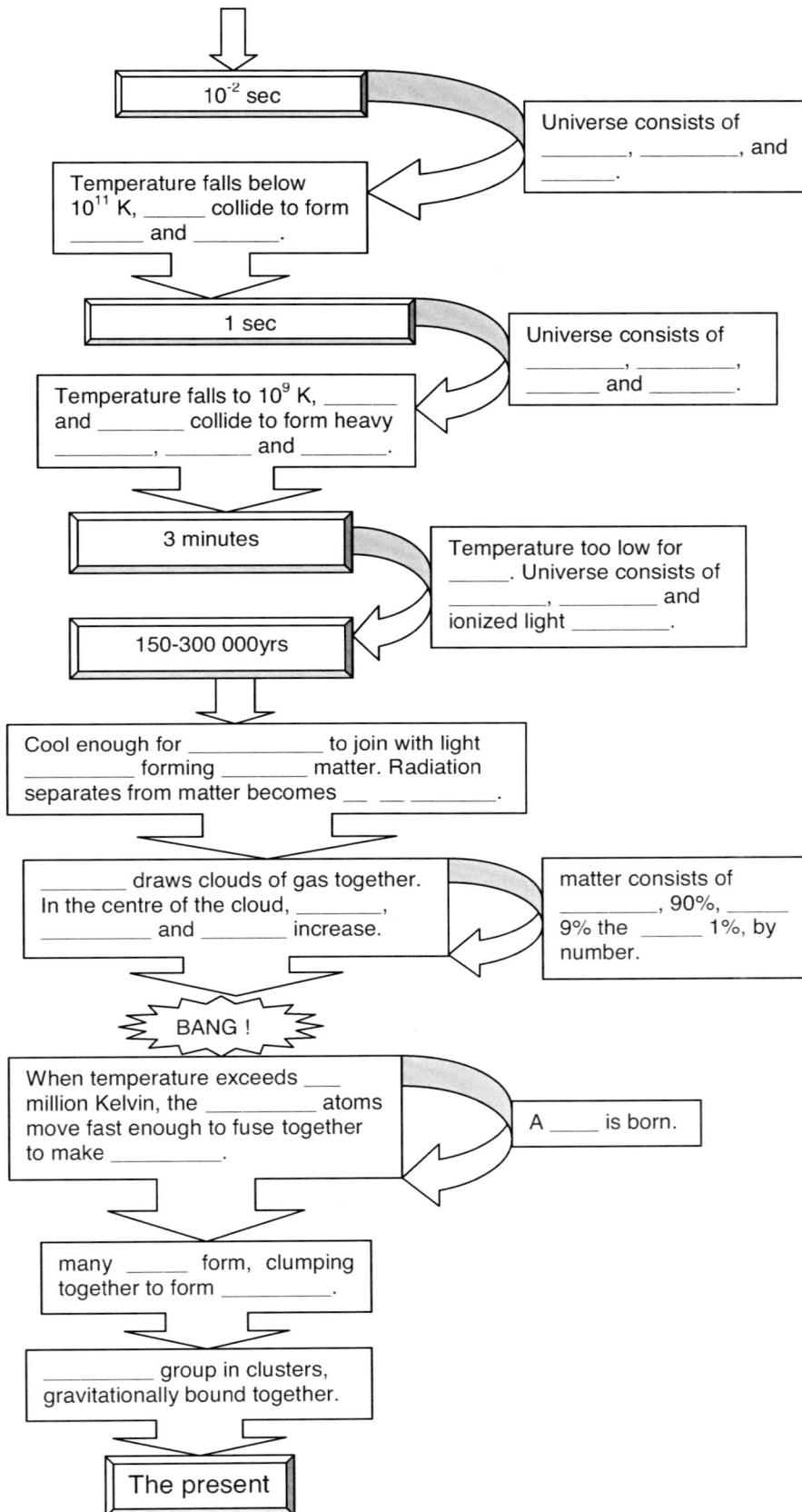

```
                    ↓
    ┌──────────────────────────┐
    │      10⁻² sec            │────┐        ┌────────────────────────┐
    └──────────────────────────┘    │        │ Universe consists of   │
                                     └──────▶│ _____, _____, and  │
    ┌──────────────────────────┐             │ _____.               │
    │ Temperature falls below  │◀────         └────────────────────────┘
    │ 10¹¹ K, _____ collide to form          
    │ _____ and _____.     │
    └──────────────────────────┘
                 ↓
    ┌──────────────────────────┐
    │        1 sec             │────┐        ┌────────────────────────┐
    └──────────────────────────┘    │        │ Universe consists of   │
                                     └──────▶│ _____, _____,      │
    ┌──────────────────────────┐             │ _____ and _____.   │
    │ Temperature falls to 10⁹ K, │◀──       └────────────────────────┘
    │ _____ and _____ collide to form heavy
    │ _____, _____ and _____.│
    └──────────────────────────┘
                 ↓
    ┌──────────────────────────┐
    │       3 minutes          │────┐        ┌────────────────────────┐
    └──────────────────────────┘    │        │ Temperature too low for│
                                     │        │ _____. Universe consists of
    ┌──────────────────────────┐    └──────▶│ _____, _____ and   │
    │      150-300 000yrs      │◀──          │ ionized light _____. │
    └──────────────────────────┘             └────────────────────────┘
                 ↓
┌────────────────────────────────────────┐
│ Cool enough for _____ to join with light
│ _____ forming _____ matter. Radiation
│ separates from matter becomes __ __ _____.│
└────────────────────────────────────────┘
                 ↓
    ┌──────────────────────────┐             ┌────────────────────────┐
    │ _____ draws clouds of gas together.   │ matter consists of     │
    │ In the centre of the cloud, _____,────┤│ _____, 90%, _____   │
    │ _____ and _____ increase.│◀──   │ 9% the _____ 1%, by   │
    └──────────────────────────┘             │ number.                │
                 ↓                            └────────────────────────┘
            ✷ BANG ! ✷
┌────────────────────────────────────────┐
│ When temperature exceeds ___            │────┐   ┌──────────────────┐
│ million Kelvin, the _____ atoms    │    │   │ A _____ is born. │
│ move fast enough to fuse together       │    └──▶└──────────────────┘
│ to make _____.                     │◀──
└────────────────────────────────────────┘
                 ↓
    ┌──────────────────────────┐
    │ many _____ form, clumping│
    │ together to form _____.│
    └──────────────────────────┘
                 ↓
    ┌──────────────────────────┐
    │ _____ group in clusters,│
    │ gravitationally bound together.│
    └──────────────────────────┘
                 ↓
    ┌──────────────────────────┐
    │      The present         │
    └──────────────────────────┘
```

Common mistakes

-units are forgotten. Remember most quantities have units, eg luminosity in Watts, brightness in Watts metre^{-2} etc. Some have no units, eg magnitude.

-incorrect units are given. Remember units can be found from the equation, eg Hubble's constant H = v/d, v in kms^{-1} and D in Mpc, so units of Hubble's constant are kms^{-1}Mpc^{-1}.

-quantities are not converted to the right units, eg, wavelength in nanometres must normally be converted to metres.

-the answer is not rounded. Remember the guideline, round to the least number of digits given in the question.

-magnitude scale is reversed. Remember a more negative magnitude means brighter.

-the spectral type scale on an HR diagram is reversed. Remember temperature decreases from left to right on the diagram.

-a requested diagram is poorly drawn. Remember; use a sharp pencil and a ruler! Such simple solutions gain valuable points.

-no working is shown. Remember that marks are given for working out and credit is possible even if the final answer is wrong.

-the sign of the apparent or absolute magnitude is confused. Often the negative sign is missed off when rearranging the formula and m-M in the distance formula remains a subtraction in spite of absolute magnitude being negative. Be careful with signs.

Core Questions

S1. What is the largest planet is the solar system?

S2. What is the closest planet to the sun?

S3. Between which planets are the asteroids found?

S4. What are comets made of?

S5. What is the name of an asymmetrical group of hundreds of stars bound together by gravity?

S6. What is the name of a spinning neutron star?

S7. What balances the force of gravity in a star and stops it collapsing?

S8. What colour is a star of spectral type O5?

S9. A star is orange in colour. What spectral type would it be?

S10. A galaxy is known to be 6.0 x 10^{22} m away. How far is this in light years?

S11. The Beehive cluster is 520 ly away. What is this in metres?

S12. A star has a surface temperature of 28 000K. What is the power output per unit area of surface?

S13. A star of luminosity 6.0x10^{28} W has a radius 3.0x10^{9}m. What is the surface temperature?

S14. A star of temperature 15 000K has a radius of 9.0 x 10^{8} m. What is the luminosity?

S15. A star of luminosity 2.0 x 10^{26} W has a surface temperature 4000K. What is its radius?

S16. A star of luminosity 4.0 x 10^{27} W is observed from a distance of 2.0 x 10^{18} m. What is the apparent brightness?

S17. A star of apparent brightness 5.0 x 10^{-8} Wm^{-2} has a luminosity 3.2 x 10^{30} W. Find its distance.

S18. A star of apparent brightness 4.0 x 10^{-7} Wm^{-2} is known to be at a distance of 7.0 x 10^{19} m. What is its luminosity?

S19. A star's black body radiation curve peaks at a wavelength of 420nm. Find its surface temperature.

S20. Mira has a surface temperature of 3600K. At what wavelength does the black body radiation curve peak?

S21. Look at the black body radiation curves on page 7. Find the wavelength at maximum intensity for the middle curve and calculate the surface temperature.

S22. Look at the graph of the eclipsing binary star on page 9. Why are alternate eclipses of different brightness? How long does an eclipse last?

S23. A star is vertically above the sun on the HR diagram. What is different about the star? What is the same?

S24. A star is horizontally to the left of the sun on the HR diagram. What is different about the star? What is the same?

S25. Take these five stars and plot them on the HR diagram on page 12. Then identify for each star which group to which they most likely belong:

Star	Sp	Mv
A	K5	-5.2
B	G8	+15.5
C	F3	-4.0
D	O2	-6.3
E	M1	-0.8

S26. A star has a parallax of 0.43". What is the distance in parsec? What is this in light years? If the parallax error is +/-0.01" what is the distance error?

S27. A star is 12pc away. What is its parallax?

S28. Two stars have apparent magnitudes of +2.5 and +4.7. Which is the brighter? How many times brighter is it?

S29. Two stars have a brightness ratio of 25. What is the magnitude difference?

S30. A star of apparent magnitude +2.8 and is 125pc away. What is the absolute magnitude?

S31. A star is 82 pc away and has an absolute magnitude of -3.2. What is its apparent magnitude?

S32. A star has an apparent magnitude of +1.4 and an absolute magnitude of –6.3. How far away is it?

S33. A Cepheid variable has a mean apparent magnitude of +6.5 and a period of 20days. Using the period luminosity graph on page 20 find its absolute magnitude? How far away is it?

S34. What is the important fact about a flat universe?

S35. What happens to the universe if it has more than the critical density?

S36. What is a MACHO?

Higher level questions

H1. What is needed to fuse four protons to make helium?

H2. What happens in the centre of a star that causes it to leave the main sequence to become a red giant?

H3. What happens to a star below the Chandrasekhar limit?

H4. List the changes of star type for a star with a mass between 1.4 solar masses and 2.5 solar masses.

H5A. What is the likely outcome for a star with a mass ten times that of the sun?

H5B. A main sequence star has a mass 8 times that of the sun. How does it's luminosity compare to that of the sun?

H6. Mention three things about the structure of the Milky Way.

H7. Name the three types of galaxies

H8. What is the difference between a galactic cluster and a supercluster?

H9. Why is the light from distant galaxies red shifted?

H10. What is Hubble's Law?

H11. The hydrogen beta line has a wavelength of 432.00nm in the lab. When measured in the spectrum of the galaxy M31, the wavelength is 430.00nm. Find the velocity of the galaxy.

H12. A galaxy in the Virgo cluster has the hydrogen alpha line (wavelength 650.000nm) at 650.325 nm. Find the recessional velocity. From the Hubble law graph on page 32 find out how far away the galaxy is.

H13. A galaxy is 8Mpc away. Using Hubble's constant as 50kms^{-1}Mpc^{-1}, find its recessional velocity. What will be the wavelength of the sodium line of 589.00nm?

H14. When Hubble first tried to measure his constant. He came up with the value of 500 kms^{-1}Mpc^{-1}. What would this value give for the age of the universe? The oldest rocks on the earth were known to be 4.7 billion years. What did Hubble's original constant imply from this?

H15. What happened to the antimatter in the universe during the Big bang?

H16. What is thought to be the cause of the Inflationary epoch?

H17. What happened to the quarks in the early universe?

H18. What allowed the electrons to unite with the nuclei to form atoms?

Answers

(Note, clues are given in the brackets)

S1. Jupiter. S2. Mercury. S3. Mars and Jupiter. S4. ice and dust. S5. open (moving) cluster. S6. pulsar. S7. radiation pressure. S8. blue S9. K. S10. 6.3 x 10^6 ly (use 1ly = 9.46 x 10^{15} m). S11. 4.9 x 10^{18} m. S12. 3.5 x 10^{10} Wm^{-2} (use L=σAT^4). S13. 9800K (use A = 4πr^2). S14. 2.9 x 10^{28} W. S15. 1.05 x 10^9 m. S16. 7.96 x 10^{-11} Wm^{-2} (use b = $\dfrac{L}{4\pi d^2}$). S17. 2.3 x 10^{10} m. S18. 2.5 x 10^{34} W. S19. 6900K (use λmax = 0.00290/T). S20. 8.1 x 10^{-7} m. S21. 5270K. S22. stars different surface brightness, eclipses last 10days. S23. more luminous, same colour/surface temp. S24. hotter surface, same luminosity. S25. A supergiant, B white dwarf, C Cepheid/giant, D main sequence, E giant. S26. 2.43+/-0.06pc (use d = 1 /p) . S27. 0.083". S28. +2.5, 7.6 (use b$_2$/b$_1$ = 2.511$^{m_1-m_2}$). S29. 3.5. S30. –2.7. S31. +1.4. S32. 350pc. S33. -4.9, 2000pc. S34. expansion rate reaches zero. S35. closed. S36. massive compact halo objects.

H1. 15 million K or more! H2. no more hydrogen fusion energy. H3. becomes a white dwarf. H4. neutron star. H5A. black hole. H5B. about 1300 times as luminous (use L = M$^{3.45}$) H6. central bulge, halo, flat (spiral) disc. H7. spiral elliptical, irregular. H8. a galactic supercluster is made up of galactic clusters. H9. they are moving away from us. H10. velocity is proportional to distance. H11. 1390kms^{-1} (use v/c = $\Delta\lambda$/λ). H12. 150kms^{-1}, 3Mpc (use v = Hd). H13. 400kms^{-1}, 589.79nm. H14. 2 billion yrs, the earth is older than the universe! (convert the H value to ms^{-1} and Mps to metres then use v=x/t to find t in seconds) H15. annihilated with the matter. H16. gravity separates from the other forces of nature. H17. joined to form protons and neutrons. H18. temperature falls below ionisation level.

THE END